SHROP
RAM]

Countryside Books' walking guides cover most areas of England and Wales and include the following series:

County Rambles
Walks For Motorists
Exploring Long Distance Paths
Literary Walks
Pub Walks

A complete list is available from the publishers:

3 Catherine Road, Newbury, Berkshire

SHROPSHIRE RAMBLES

Twenty Three Country Walks
around Shropshire

Robert Smart

———

With Historical Notes

COUNTRYSIDE BOOKS
NEWBURY, BERKSHIRE

COUNTRYSIDE BOOKS
3 Catherine Road
Newbury, Berkshire

ISBN 1 85306 184 0

Cover photograph of The Vale of Clun
taken by Bill Meadows

Produced through MRM Associates Ltd., Reading
Typeset by Paragon Typesetters, Sandycroft, Chester
Printed in England by J. W. Arrowsmith Ltd., Bristol

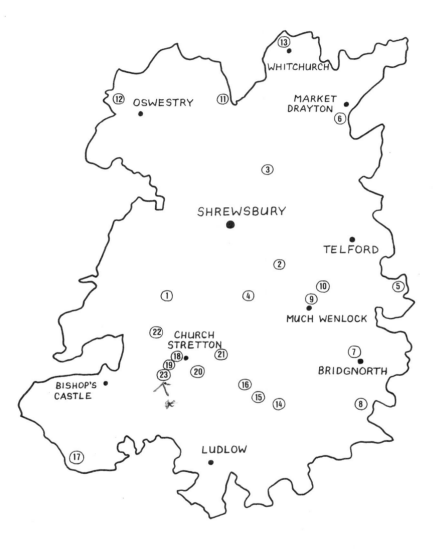

WHITCHURCH
⑬

OSWESTRY ⑫ ⑪

MARKET
DRAYTON
⑥

③

SHREWSBURY

TELFORD

②

⑤

① ④ ⑩
⑨

MUCH WENLOCK

CHURCH
STRETTON
⑱
⑲ ⑳ ㉑
㉓ ㉒

BISHOP'S
CASTLE

⑦

BRIDGNORTH

⑯
⑮ ⑭
⑧

⑰

LUDLOW

Sketch map showing locations of the walks.

Contents

COUNTRY CODE

1. Guard against all risks of fire.
2. Fasten all gates.
3. Keep dogs under proper control.
4. Keep to the paths across farmland.
5. Avoid damaging fences.
6. Leave no litter.
7. Safeguard water supplies
8. Protect wild life, wild plants and trees.
9. Go carefully on country roads.
10. Respect the life of the countryside.

Introduction

Shropshire is described in several guides to England as the most beautiful of English counties. It is certainly one of the least spoilt. Being beyond the ever stretching tentacles of the London sprawl, although not far from the Birmingham conurbation as the crow flies, it has nonetheless, apart from Telford, escaped large scale developments and remains a quiet and beautiful county in which to find rest and repose. The walks vary from the wild windswept uplands of south Shropshire to the calm canalside walks at Ellesmere and Whitchurch. Shropshire is certainly a county of contrasts.

The southern part of the county is dominated by the Stretton Hills, the last vestiges of the Welsh Mountains which spill over into the English border counties. The Longmynd is a mecca for all serious walkers and the casual rambler while the other hills in the area offer in their different ways their own particular attractions. Wenlock Edge, immortalized in song and verse, stretches north-east/south-west across the area while the Clee Hills give Shropshire the distinction of having the highest peaks south of the Pennines.

The river Severn cuts the county into two and north of it we come to the Shropshire Plain, interrupted here and there by rocky outcrops such as Haughmond Hill and Grinshill. The longest stretch of any canal within a single county boundary cuts across the northern part of the county and affords some enjoyable walks while the area to the south-west of the A5 around Oswestry is entirely untouched by the 20th century and a walk there is rather like stepping back into a bygone age, such is the peace and tranquillity one finds there.

Shrewsbury itself is a most attractive county town and even recent developments have been made with taste and decorum as befits a town of its character. Being in the centre of the county, directions to the start of all walks are based on starting from there. Other market towns worthy of closer examination are Ludlow, Oswestry, Whitchurch, Much Wenlock and Market Drayton, all of which are included in this book.

The short historical notes given at the end of each walk provide some information about the places visited and what to look out for. The sketch map that accompanies each walk is designed to guide walkers to the starting point and give a simple yet accurate idea of the route to be taken. To enable you to enjoy the benefit of detailed maps the number of the relevant Ordnance Survey 1:50 000 Landranger map is given for each walk, in addition to a grid reference for the starting point.

No special equipment is needed to enjoy the countryside on foot, but do wear a stout pair of shoes and remember that at least one muddy patch is likely even on the sunniest day. Please remember the Country Code and make sure that gates are not left open or any farm animals disturbed.

Many hours of enjoyment have gone into preparing these walks. I hope the reader will find great pleasure in them too.

Robert Smart
Spring 1992

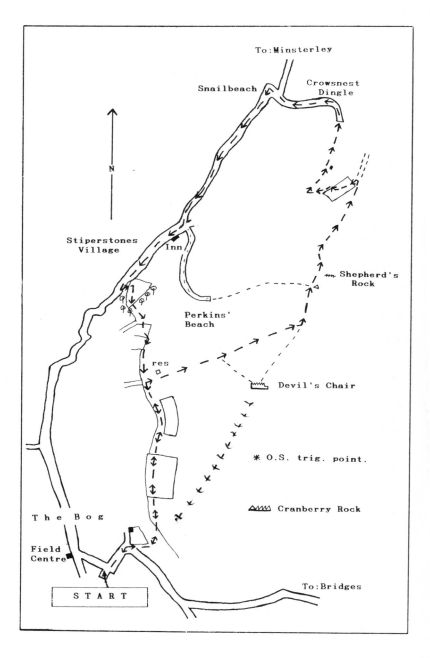

To:Minsterley

Snailbeach

Crowsnest
Dingle

N

Stiperstones
Village

Inn

Shepherd's
Rock

Perkins'
Beach

res

Devil's Chair

* O.S. trig. point.

Cranberry Rock

The Bog

Field
Centre

To:Bridges

START

+ ALTERNATIVE WALK.

The Stiperstones

Introduction: This walk is noted for its fabulous views. The Stiperstones is long and narrow yet wherever one is on this walk there are superb views, first to the west and south, then to the east and north. The Stiperstones has some of the best heather in Shropshire and unlike the Longmynd is not nearly so troubled by bracken. It is also a marvellous place to come bilberry picking (blueberries/whinberries) especially near the Devil's Chair. This is an area rich in folklore and legend. The walk is on the level on wide clear tracks as far as Shepherd's Rock with a gentle descent to Snailbeach. The only uphill stretch is coming back from Stiperstones village.

Distance: 5 miles (allow three hours without stops for the full walk). Map — OS Landranger 137.

Refreshments: The Stiperstones Inn, near the phone box in Stiperstones village. Bar meals available and outdoor tables. Children are welcome. It is perfectly located for this walk!

How to get there: The walk commences at 'The Bog' where the site of a former lead mine has been converted into a large car park. From Shrewsbury take the A488 south-west through Pontesbury to Minsterley and a mile beyond fork left to Snailbeach and continue along a minor road to The Bog, the car park is sharp left about 100 yards up the road. (GR 979358).

The Walk: Turn right uphill out of the car park as far as the Z bend where there is a waymarked stile. Skirt the adjacent field, as waymarked, and turn half-left still going uphill, to a stile in the top left-hand corner. Once over the stile you will be at NNC post 3. These posts, with their detailed maps, will be encountered often and the maps are an invaluable help on the walk as an added source of guidance.

A wide path bears half-left through the heather and crossing two stiles on either end of former fields, a well defined track begins. The views around are excellent, the hill to your left is Corndon Hill and in the far distance is the flat outline of Plynlimon and due west the craggy bulk of Cader Idris, both on the Welsh coast. To the south the Black Mountains can be seen.

After emerging from a wide grassy track between fields you again have heather on your right. At the track crossroads, by a green-fenced reservoir with fire-beaters outside, turn right onto a wide track between heather and head towards a large outcrop of rocks known as the Devil's Chair. There are more fine views left as you gain the higher ground and you can see Stiperstones village below you at the foot of Perkins Beach with the Welsh Mountains to the west. (If you wish to go up to the Chair you will see two parallel paths, vehicle tracks, going straight towards it. Once there turn left to rejoin the walk.)

At the next crossroads of tracks north of the Chair turn left along the hilltop with superb views ahead to the north. The hill in the middle distance is the Wrekin and to the east is the low flat top of the Longmynd. The next junction of paths is marked by a large pile of rocks and a short cut can be taken by turning left and following a well defined track to Stiperstones village where you rejoin the walk at the phone box.

The main walk continues along the top, soon dropping downhill to a lone field. Turn left at the far end and then left again through a bridle gate. Cross the field bearing slightly right and through a line of trees, where turn right to the now visible stile. Turn left along the outside of the fence for no more than 5 yards and find an indistinct track through the heather. At a fork of tracks go right and ahead you will see a bank of fire-beaters, so head that way. At the crossroads of paths turn right down the valley and turn left on reaching the road. Follow the road to Stiperstones village, with its phone box, shop and inn.

As you leave the village watch for the word 'slow' painted on the road by a Z road sign. At the top of the bank on your left is a waymarked stile. Go over and turn right uphill alongside the wood. Ignore the first stile across the field to your left, carry on ahead until you come to a waymarked stile and NNR sign 7. Continue uphill, ignore a path on the right, until you come to a field, a stile, and sign 6. Cross the stile and field to a gate in the far corner and sign 5. Turn right along the track back to your car.

Historical Notes

The Stiperstones and The Devil have been inextricably linked for centuries. The Devil's Chair has more legends than anywhere else in Britain. When low rain clouds close in and the hilltop is lost in the mist, he returns to sit in his chair and in former times the locals would stay indoors with the shutters up. When the clouds lift he prowls round his chair waiting for the mist to return. It is said that anybody sitting in his chair will be cursed. On the shortest day of the year all the ghosts of the local dead meet around his chair to choose their King, and anyone abroad that night who witnesses this event is stricken with fear and often does not live the year.

The area south from the Chair is peppered with loose rocks and boulders which make walking very difficult. The legend is that the Devil was crossing the hill on his way from Ireland with his apron full of rocks with which he intended filling the valleys. He sat down to rest in his chair but when he stood up his apron string broke and the rocks were scattered as you see them still.

Another legend is that once the Devil got a stone in his shoe and sat down in his chair to flick it out. It landed in a field near Bishops Castle. When the church clock struck 13 the stone turned round! He must take a large size in shoe for the stone was a good 20 ft round!

Edric the Wild: Another figure of local folklore is Edric the Wild, or the

Forester as some call him. A few years before the coming of William the Conqueror, Edric was hunting in the wild, mountainous country in the Forest of Clun. He became separated from his companions and, as dusk was falling, saw a mysterious light which led him to a strange building. The light came from a window and, looking through, Edric saw 'seven beautiful maidens all robed in white and dancing hand in hand'. He fell in love with the youngest and most beautiful of the maidens and, rushing to the door, burst it open and seized her in his arms. The other maidens instantly changed into fierce beasts and attacked him tooth and claw, but holding his precious burden aloft Edric fought his way out and galloped away. For three months the lovely and mysterious wife of the wild forester spoke no word until one day, wishing him well, she promised to be true as long as he never made mention of her sisters or the place from which he snatched her. Her name was Godda and they lived happily for many years but then, one day, Edric, because he was kept waiting for his meal, forgot and in his rough wild way blamed Godda for her sisters and shouted 'It is your sisters who have kept me waiting!' And at this, with a sad look of remorse she disappeared and he never saw her again. Nobody ever heard that he died a natural death and the legend says that he sleeps under the Stiperstones awaiting judgement day. The lead miners used to say they could hear his men 'tapping' in the underground caverns and that when they did they would find a new rich seam of lead. His only release is before war when he and his wild huntsmen, with Godda at his side, ride across the hill. He was seen, alone, on the Longmynd before the Second World War.

The mines: Lead was first mined in the area in the time of the Romans, but the mines did not come of age until the end of the 18th century when activity in the region was at its height. It tailed off in the 19th century when prices fell and geological difficulties forced closures, but those mines which did continue were very prosperous to the extent of, at one time, producing around ten per cent of the nation's needs in lead ore. Little of them now remains but one can still find old winding houses, slag heaps and fenced off shafts.

The Bog: Not a very pretty name but it was just that before an underground drain was built in the late 18th century. As recently as the early 19th century the area was quite a good sized industrial area with its mines, houses, pubs etc. Now only the school remains and the pub, which is now a private dwelling.

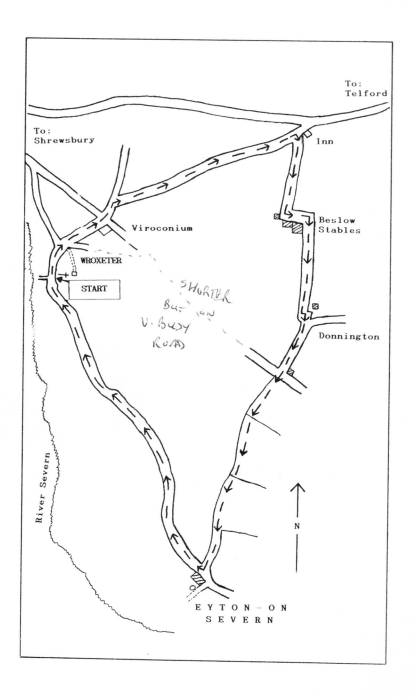

To:
Telford

To:
Shrewsbury

Inn

Viroconium

Beslow
Stables

WROXETER

START

SHORTER
BUT ON
V. BUSY
ROAD

Donnington

River Severn

N

EYTON - ON
SEVERN

SEPT 23 2014 — JENNY

WALK TWO

Wroxeter, Roman Viroconium and Eyton-on-Severn

Introduction: A quiet and easy walk through the quiet backwaters of rural Shropshire, set in a corner almost forgotten by the 20th century. Sumptuous views are afforded throughout especially on the first and last stretches. It is also a walk through an area steeped in history and includes the site of the Roman baths at Viroconium, the largest Roman city to have escaped subsequent development.

Distance: 5 miles, allow three hours without stops. Map — OS Landranger 126.

Refreshments: The Wroxeter Hotel, immediately behind and linked to the church, the Horsehoes Inn halfway round the walk, and at Atcham The Mytton & Mermaid.

How to get there: Wroxeter is 5 miles south-east of Shrewsbury. Leave Shrewsbury on the A5 (from autumn 1992 it will be the B4380) passing Atcham and beyond Attingham House and Park fork right into a minor road signposted Ironbridge. About 200 yards farther fork right into a narrow lane. Park opposite the church at Wroxeter. (GR 565084).

The Walk: From the church walk back along the lane as far as the entrance to the Wroxeter Hotel where you continue ahead, ignoring the lanes to left and right. As you walk you will see to your right the Wrekin hill, and away to your left in the distance is Atcham. As you approach the English Heritage centre at Viroconium look to the left as well as to the right as there are Roman remains on both sides of the lane.   *—100 YDS AFTER X ROADS*

At the crossroads go straight ahead as signposted 'Norton ½', passing the village shop, and in 100 yards fork right into a narrow lane. This lane skirts round the north-west edge of Viroconium and English Heritage signs will be seen on the gates. To your left in the distance is Haughmond Hill.

Turn right across the car park of the Horsehoes Inn, well situated for a halfway stop, and take a narrow lane beyond the car park's left-hand corner. Follow this lane for a mile, passing around Beslow Stables after which the track is sandy and grassy. The Wrekin is close now on your left and beyond the stables a fine view stretches south to the Stretton Hills, with Lawley and Caradoc on the left and the low bulk of the Longmynd across the horizon to

CLOSED AND POST BOX ON WALL

15

the right. At the end of the track, turn left then right by a large red-brick farmhouse and join the lane by a letter box. Go straight ahead.

At the T junction by a half-timbered house, cross the road and go through the left of two facing gates onto a wide grassy track which skirts three fields before becoming a hedged-in lane just before Eyton-on-Severn. The track you are walking from the Horseshoes Inn to Eyton was once the main road from Wellington to Acton Burnell.

On reaching the lane by the farm at Eyton, turn right and walk back along this lane to Wroxeter. As you do so, you will have excellent views south across the Severn Valley and north to the Wrekin, which never seems far away on this walk. This road is deceptive in that it is higher than one would think, hence the lovely views afforded by it in the southerly direction.

Historical Notes

Viroconium: The name Wroxeter appears to mean 'the fort by the Wrekin'. When the Romans came they built a large fortified town where Watling Street, the present A5, crossed the Severn before proceeding south to Hereford. Viroconium, as the Romans called it, was the fourth largest city built in England after London, St Albans and Cirencester. Much of the church is built from stone taken from the Roman buildings. The entrance to the churchyard is through a gateway flanked by two Roman columns and the font is also fashioned from a Roman pillar.

Viroconium is the largest Roman city to have escaped subsequent development. Most of the city is now under fields but the impressive bath house remains. At its height the city covered an area of 180 acres. The Emperor Hadrian visited it in AD 122 and set into motion an ambitious building and fortification programme. The city was a bustling commercial as well as military centre and traders from many parts of Europe came to set up businesses in its busy streets. It was from here that Ostorius Scapula, the second Roman Governor of Britain, sallied forth to battle against King Caractacus.

The importance of Viroconium as a frontier fortification can be seen as you walk back from Eyton-on-Severn to Wroxeter, as the outer defences were built where now is the road and the added defence given by the close proximity of the river Severn made this an easily defendable location. It was the Emperor Nero who deciding to subdue the Welsh, gave Viroconium its great military importance as a forward base.

Eyton-on-Severn: There is an interesting tower dating back to the days of Henry VIII. To see it, turn left on reaching the lane then right into a public footpath (ignore 'Private Road' sign). I was told there were formerly four such towers and that they were used as lodging houses. It is now let out as a holiday home.

WALKED WITH JENNY
SEPT 26 2014 PARKED
NEAR CHURCH IN CLIVE
AND SHORTENED WALK

Yorton
and Grinshill

Introduction: Surrounded by the low lying and rich grasslands of the North Shropshire Plain the sandstone outcrop of Grinshill is like an island surrounded by the sea, but what is more striking about it is the complete contrast in vegetation, including an area very reminiscent of Hampshire's New Forest. The walk starts from Yorton so as to give the walker a more striking impression of this contrast and also to give you time to appreciate the beauty of the hill as you approach it from the west. An easy walk mostly on level ground and suitable for all ages.

Distance: 4 miles, allow three hours. Map — OS Landranger 126.

Refreshments: The Railway Inn, Yorton, and meals at the Elephant and Castle at Grinshill which is roughly halfway.

How to get there: Grinshill is situated 7 miles north of Shrewsbury. By car — drive north out of Shrewsbury on the A49 Whitchurch road. Two miles north of Hadnall watch for a concealed left turn signposted Yorton and Clive. Follow the signs to Yorton and park at Yorton station. (GR 505238). By train — there is a good service from Shrewsbury and Crewe/Whitchurch to Yorton, the trains being nicely spaced so as to give adequate time for the walk.

The Walk: Turn right out of the station yard. After passing the red-brick farmhouse on the left (built 1886) you can, over the stone wall, already see the striking spire of Clive church. Turn left through the first gate on the left. The spire of Clive church is directly ahead and a good landmark. Cross the field keeping just left of a wooden electricity pylon beyond which is a sort of stile. Cross the small paddock beyond it and go straight ahead into a long narrow field where you immediately go over a stile on your right into a large field. Using the spire as a guide go straight up the field heading directly for the church and at the top you will come to two facing gates, side by side. Go through the gate on the left.
  On emerging from the track in Clive, turn right for the church and then left passing in front of the church. Turn right by the church gate and find the bridleway, a steep and rocky track going uphill alongside a high wall and known locally as 'The Glat', an old Shropshire word meaning a path or alley. At the top of this rise pass the school built in 1873 and here the track opens out on a narrow plateau, ideal for picnics and an area very reminiscent of the

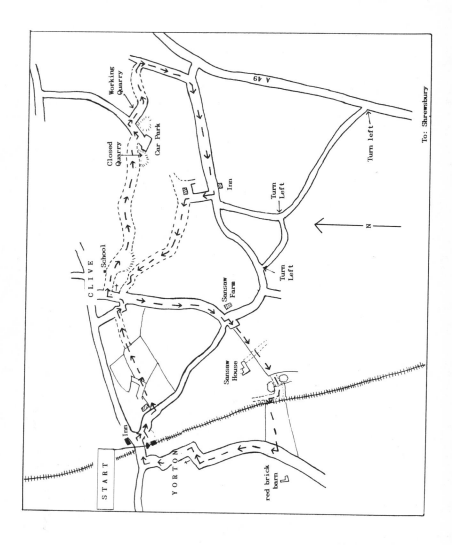

New Forest, with its silver birches, pines and bracken and with an excellent viewpoint looking south towards Shrewsbury and beyond to the Stretton Hills. The long low hill in the distance with a pointed bit in the middle is Caradoc and to the east is the volcano-shaped hill of the Wrekin.

Continue on the track, now level with fine views north over the Shropshire Plain, for a mile, passing several side tracks. After passing a cottage you join, ~~for a short distance~~, the Shropshire Way marked with the 'buzzard' sign. At the road, turn left, and then in a few yards, turn right. This new road peters out by some cottages and drops downhill through the woods emerging on level ground into a new lane. Turn right at the next junction and walk along the lane into Grinshill passing the manor house Stone Grange just before The ~~Elephant and Castle~~. A little way beyond the inn turn right, signed 'Village Hall'.

By the village hall, bear left and follow a sunken track with a wall on the left and pine trees on the slopes on the right. There are a few houses along this track and more views south across the Shropshire Plain. On reaching Clive church again, turn left and walk along the lane for ½ mile. At a T junction turn left and then immediately opposite Sansaw Farm, right, by the public footpath signpost towards Sansaw House. There are two gates facing you. Go through the gate on the left and using the park fence as a guide, cross the park in front of the house until your enter a small wooded area. Cross the bridge and then the railway by the white fence. Heading towards the farm on the far hillside come to the lane and turn right for Yorton.

Historical Notes

Clive: The spire is on a most impressive church built into the side of the hill, or cliffe, from which the village takes its name, and is a landmark for miles around. There has been a church here since Norman times and parts of the original 12th century building can still be seen. The village is exceptionally pretty, most of the houses and the high walls being built of local stone. The centre of the village is a conservation area and a walk round its tidy streets is very rewarding. Copper mines were also worked at Clive from Roman times and vast tunnels still extend underneath most of the village. The main shaft is still in use to hold water which supplies the farms and cottages on the Sansaw estate and produces some 25,000 gallons a day. The copper mines closed in 1886.

Grinshill: The area has been quarried for sandstone since Roman times, who used the stone to build Viroconium. The stone can also be seen in many of Shrewsbury's major buildings and the door surrounds of No 10 Downing Street. Visitors can see stone being worked. In its heyday, great slabs of stone, weighing as much as 14 tons each, were hewn from its face, some to be sent as far away as the United States. The summit of Grinshill is 630 ft and the quarry passed on the north side of the hill some 200 ft deep. The manor house, Stone Grange, which is Jacobean is locally known as 'The Pest House'. The village hall was originally a school but when the school at Clive was built its use changed first to a Sunday school and then to its present day function.

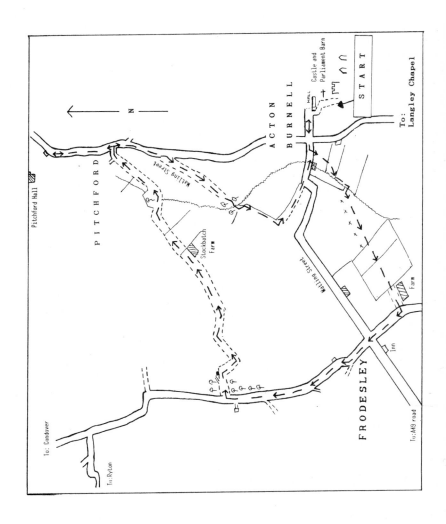

N

Pitchford Hall

To: Condover

To: Ryton

PITCHFORD

Watling Street

Stockbatch Farm

ACTON BURNELL

HALL

Castle and Parliament Barn

START

To: Langley Chapel

Watling Street

Farm

FRODESLEY

Inn

To: A49 road

Acton Burnell and Pitchford

Introduction: A superb rural walk through fields, along quiet lanes, and as level as a country walk will ever be. Throughout the walk one gets outstanding views in all directions in an area noted for its tranquillity. The walk takes in such diverse places as the site of England's first Parliament, a Roman road and the foremost Tudor residence in England.

Distance: 5 miles (allow three hours' walking). Map — OS Landranger 126.

Refreshments: The Swan Inn, Frodesley, or the Fox Inn at Ryton.

How to get there: Acton Burnell is situated to the south-east of Shrewsbury. Take the A49 south from Shrewsbury through Dorrington and turn left at the signpost to Longnor. Drive through Longnor and turn left at the crossroads beyond the village, signposted Acton Burnell. In Acton Burnell go straight ahead at the crossroads signposted 'Castle' and on the approach to Acton Burnell Hall (occasionally open) turn right through what at first appears to be the gate pillars to somebody's drive. Park inside anywhere opposite or near the church. (GR 530020).

The Walk: Before starting out you may want to visit the church, the castle and beyond that the site of England's first Parliament. Entrance to the latter two is along the dirt track beyond the church, and it is signed. In the field beyond the castle you will see two ends of what might have been a Norman barn. It is here that Edward I called together England's first Parliament in 1295.

From the car park, return to the village. Go over at the crossroads signposted 'Frodesley 1', pass the post office and the Old School House. Just beyond this, where the footpath ends is a public footpath sign and two stiles, one beyond the other. Cross the field diagonally to a field gate and the second field likewise, the gate here is by the hedge on the right. In the third field keep alongside the hedge until you come to a footbridge. Cross the stream. The next field is very large with no obvious footpath but use the electricity pylons as a compass and keeping approximately 10 yards to the left of them, cross the field. Notice the Stretton Hills straight ahead of you. The hill you can see in the centre of the view is Lawley which from this angle blots out the higher bulk of Caradoc beyond it. Some 10 yards left of the last pylon is a stile. Now go straight ahead through three fields to the barns at the farm and turn right in the lane to Frodsham.

At the crossroads in Frodsham, by the telephone box, go straight ahead as signposted 'Condover' and walk along the lane for 1 mile with lovely views south. From here Caradoc can now be seen. Pass a 'Ford' road sign and then a Z road sign to turn right at the foot of the hill onto a rough track which starts by the public bridleway sign. This track is wide and clear right to Stockbatch Farm and I am sure you will enjoy the wonderful views on every side along this track. In the distance is the Wrekin hill, and to the north-east you can just see the tops of, and the steam from, the cooling towers at Buildwas power station.

Go straight ahead at the farm to a facing gate beyond the barn. The track is now inside fields but continues ahead as before, passing through several gates but always clearly defined. In a dip you pass over a stream and past a small copse before a short rise. The track eventually arrives at Pitchford village.

Turn left for a short two-way detour. Walk out the other end of the village as far as the lodge gates from where you get a superb view of the most famous Tudor mansion in Shropshire. It is occasionally open to the public.

Now return through the village back the way you came, passing the bridleway and walking out the other end. Pass an S bend sign, and at the next bend, just beyond where 'slow' has been painted in the road, leave the road and go straight ahead along a grassy track. This is part of the Roman road from Wroxeter (Viroconium) to Kenchester, Hereford, and is called Watling Street and is one of the best stretches, going in an almost direct line for a good mile. Cross the stream by a footbridge and bear slightly left in the field alongside a fence, and then right alongside a hedge (on your left) as far as a tarmac track, where you turn left and then it's straight enough back to Acton Burnell.

Historical Notes

Acton Burnell gets its name from two sources, Ac-tune meaning Oak-town, and Burnell from Robert Burnell who, in the 13th century, was Bishop of Bath and Wells. It was he who built the fortified manor house. The church of St Mary is a sea of daffodils in spring. Acton Burnell Hall, occasionally open to the public, is a further education college for foreign students. From the Second World War it was used by the Sisters of the Order of Sion as a girls' school, until 1970 when it remained empty for a time until being converted to its present use.

Frodesley, believe it or not, lies on a coal seam which underlies the clay to the north and west. A brickworks nearby produced tiles and drainpipes as well as bricks, and the remains of marl pits, now ponds, still exist. In 1724 the village was quite prosperous boasting a smithy, a carpenter, a cooper, two shoemakers and a tailor, now everything has gone save for a small garage.

Watling Street: The Roman road from Wroxeter to Kenchester, here the metalled road coming from Acton Burnell direction, to your right, towards Church Stretton, to your left, and running almost as straight as a dye. True our Anglo-Saxon road builders have put in the occasional bend to break the monotony as is seen at either end of Pitchford village, but in the main it is as true today as it was 2,000 years ago. The best stretch of it is on the walk after leaving Pitchford.

Pitchford Hall: The border counties of England with Wales are renowned for their black and white, or half-timbered, buildings. This came about as a result of the local lack of building materials in the Middle Ages, such as stone, the only materials readily to hand being timber and mud. These were combined to construct the buildings we see today although, in most cases, the mud infilling between the timbers has long since been replaced by brick usually plastered over and painted white. Of all the buildings in these border counties none is so striking as Pitchford Hall. Standing almost alone amidst its parkland, Pitchford Hall can be truly admired as an outstanding example of Tudor architecture. The approach to the house is along a fine avenue of limes to the church and the latter is always open. In 1990 the Hall was opened to the public for the first time. Details of opening times can be obtained from Mrs Colthurst at the Hall, telephone (0694) 731205.

The house contains a priest's hole constructed in the early 17th century by Thomas Ottley whose son, Francis was knighted by Charles I and became Governor of Shrewsbury during the Civil War. When Catholicism was banned services were illicitly held here and as a signal to come to Mass a large white sheet would be draped prominently over a bush in the grounds.

Pitchford is an apt name which truly reflects its meaning, pitch being a black sticky substance seeping from the coal measures which underly this area. It infiltrates into a well from which it was drawn and used to coat the wooden part of the structure of the hall and other similar buildings. The ford is just that, a crossing of the Row Brook.

TONG   NEARBY IS PICTURESQUE

Boscobel
and Bishops Wood

Introduction: A walk in east Shropshire, slightly spilling over into neighbouring Staffordshire. For Shropshire it is a rather unusual walk as the countryside with its rolling, densely wooded but gentle hills is more akin to Surrey and Kent. An easy walk on the level occasionally using quiet lanes but mainly on footpaths and giving fine views. It is an area rich in English history for it was here that Charles II escaped from his pursuers after the battle of Worcester by hiding in an oak tree.

Distance: 4¼ miles, allow three hours without stops. Map — OS Landranger 127.

Refreshments: Light lunches and teas at Boscobel House. The Royal Oak Inn on the walk does very good hot and cold meals which makes a welcome halfway break.

How to get there: The walk starts at Boscobel House. From Shrewsbury, drive east on the A5 joining the M54 as far as junction 3, the turn off for Whitchurch A41. Turn left at the roundabout and head north for a mile, take the second turning right and follow the signs for Boscobel House. (GR 838082).

The Walk: Walk south-west from the car park along a narrow and quiet country lane signposted 'White Ladies Priory'. After a mile, turn right into a wood by a further sign. A wide track runs through the heart of the wood. White Ladies Priory is through the second gate on the left.

On leaving the priory grounds, turn left and continue along the now narrowing track which ends at a wicket gate marked with a blue arrow indicating a bridleway. Continue ahead alongside the hedge on the right. The buildings of Meashill Farm come into view as you walk up the field. Go through the next gate and bear right to a wide track where you turn left.

Depending on circumstances you can either go ahead at the farmyard as far as three small circular silos where you turn right onto a new track, or, if the farmyard is busy with cattle etc, you can cut across the field outside the flimsy barbed wire fence which surrounds the yard and meet the new track on the other side.

The way ahead is quite clear, you go through two sets of double gates turning left in front of a third set. Pass White Oak Farm and caravan site to the lane beyond. Turn right, then in 50 yards turn left. As you pass the next farm you

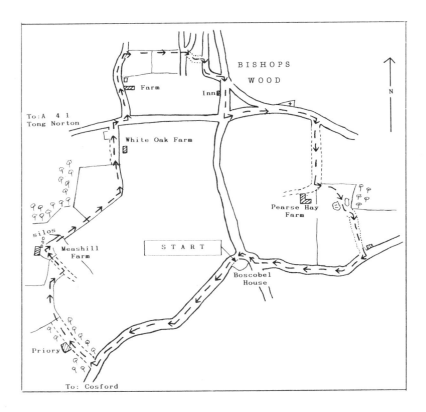

cross the county boundary from Shropshire into Staffordshire. Pass a bungalow and continue along the lane. Fifty yards past two facing gates on either side of the lane find a short flight of wooden steps leading up the bank on the right to a stile. A clearly defined footpath leads dead ahead through two fields and emerges in the village of Bishops Wood by a children's play area.

Cross Brookside Gardens half-right to a narrow footpath opposite, between two garden fences; the footpath sign is partially obscured. The path winds between several houses to emerge onto a new road by a house called The Old Inn Cottage. Turn right and in 50 yards you will come to a main road on the edge of the village. Turn right along Ivesty Bank and The Royal Oak is just a few yards further on.

From the inn continue ahead to the next crossroads. Turn left as signposted to Kiddemore Green (you will probably recognise this crossroads as being the way you drove here, and although Boscobel House is, as signposted, straight on, it is a busy road not really suited to walkers). At the next road junction fork right into Old Coach Road and pass the church.

Turn right at a farm track signed Pearse Hay Farm and follow this nearly to

25

the farm. On the right-hand bend just before the barns, turn left through a field gate onto a wide track which leads towards the woods. On reaching the next lane by a red-brick cottage, turn right. This is a very quiet lane and has some pleasant views to the right across the fields. On reaching the main road turn right for Boscobel House. Cross the road with care, it is rather busy.

Historical Notes

Boscobel House: In 1649 after seven years of civil war, Charles I was executed before his Palace in Whitehall. The heir, Charles II had fled to Holland and in 1650 returned in a desperate attempt to regain the throne. After his defeat by the Roundheads at Worcester in 1651 Charles II became a fugitive and was compelled to run for his life. Thus he came to this area. His first hiding place was White Ladies Priory and when forced to flee from there he came to Boscobel. In those days the house was a remote hunting lodge surrounded by deep forest and by day Charles hid in the branches of an oak tree and at night crept back into the house. Thus it was that while hiding in the oak, the troops of the Commonwealth arrived and searched the house, even riding beneath the very tree in which the King was hiding. Eventually he reached the Continent and after his Restoration the story of his escape became one of the most famous episodes in English history, to which so many public houses still bear witness. In 1988 Lord Montagu of Beaulieu, a descendant of King Charles II, officially reopened Boscobel after English Heritage's refurnishing and restoration. The house still boasts the 'sacred hole' in which the King is said to have spent the night. The oak tree in the gardens is not the original oak which, after the Restoration, was hacked about by the souvenir hunters of the day, but the present oak is a direct descendant and is itself nearly 300 years old. There is a gift shop and cafe.

White Ladies Priory: The Augustinian nunnery, dedicated to St Leonard, was founded in the 12th century. It stood within the Royal Forest of Brewood, some remains of which are still scattered about this area and will be seen on the walk from time to time. The name refers to the wearing of undyed habits in comparison with another nearby nunnery known as 'Blackladies'. The priory was dissolved in 1536 when it became a private dwelling.

The Royal Oak Inn — what other name could it have! There is an interesting plaque over the bar which reads 'We carried up with us some bread, cheese and beer, and got up into a great oak . . . Charles II, 1651'.

Market Drayton and Blore Heath

Introduction: Market Drayton is a small compact market town in the north-east corner of the county on the border with Staffordshire. Islanded by the surrounding rural area, it has some pleasing buildings dating back to the 17th century. This walk traverses a very pleasant agricultural area just across the border in Staffordshire, an easy walk on level ground suitable for any time of year, for all ages and almost any kind of footwear. Sumptuous views are afforded from time to time as you skirt and then cross the site of the battle of Blore Heath, fought in 1459 during the Wars of the Roses.

Distance: 4½ miles, allow two and a half hours. Map — OS Landranger 127.

Refreshments: None on the walk, the nearest inn is the Four Alls on the Market Drayton/Newport road (A529).

How to get there: Market Drayton is 12 miles north-east of Shrewsbury, by the A49 for 1 mile then A53 signposted Newcastle. Using the by-pass continue as signposted Newcastle for ½ mile beyond Market Drayton, and watch for the first turning right (unclassified road) signposted Almington. At Almington, turn right for Hales. Halfway, notice a road junction with the sign pointing right 'Four Alls 2½'; if you want refreshment that leads directly to the inn, otherwise continue to Hales and park near the church (GR 713340).

The Walk: Walk straight ahead past the church heading east. At the first junction of roads, with a grassy triangle in the middle, turn left along a short length of pavement. Go straight on at the next junction towards a red-brick house, leaving the metalled road behind and joining a concrete track which soon narrows. Just by the concrete water trough is the site of a Roman villa (in the field on the right). Continue along this track. As you approach The Nook Farm look to your right at the view which stretches south across the north Shropshire plain as far as the Stretton Hills.
   At a T junction, turn left as signed Park Springs, and at the entrance to the farm turn right towards Knowleswood. The concrete track ends here, and so turn left onto a grassy track.
   On nearing Burntwood Farm go through the facing gate and bear slightly right between two hawthorn bushes onto the track, which now continues as a sunken track across the field to the gate ahead. The stile there is no use at all.

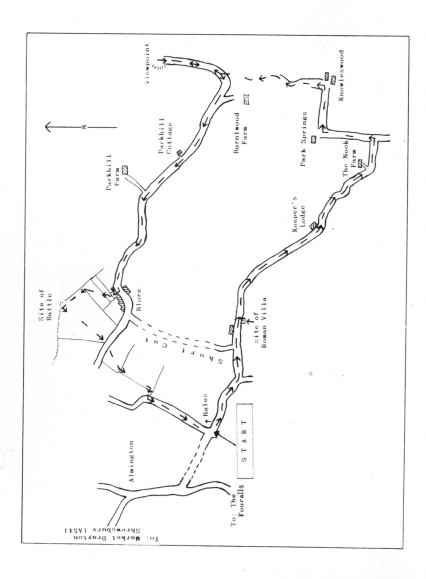

The track continues alongside the hedge, on your left, and is easily discernible. Ignore the first field gate, and join the lane at the second gate.

Turn right along a rising track which leaves a pine wood on your right and comes to a good viewpoint after about five minutes' walking. Stop and look left across some truly unspoilt countryside. In the near distance you look down on the site where the battle of Blore Heath was fought. Turn back now and retrace your steps, passing the gate through which you reached the lane and continue round to the right shortly joining a track which soon becomes a metalled lane. Continue along here for a mile until arriving at Blore Farm.

Turn right between a wooden chicken house and a red sandstone wall. Pass round the back of the chicken house where you will find a stile. Over the stile fork half-left to a second stile clearly visible with yellow tops to the side posts. Likewise cross the next field diagonally heading towards a stile in the far right-hand corner near a wooden electricity pylon. There is a row of houses dead ahead in the distance. Cross the next stile, also with yellow tops and walk alongside the hedge (on the right). You are now crossing the actual field where the battle of Blore Heath was fought.

At the bottom of the field is another stile with yellow tops and beyond it a stream, Hemp Mill Brook. Do not cross, but instead turn left at right angles to the way you came, and go back up the field using a double pylon as a guide. Keep heading towards it and just beyond come to yet another yellow topped stile which gives onto the lane.

Cross the lane to another stile immediately opposite. Cross the new field heading towards another wooden electricity pylon and a stile in the far right-hand corner, also waymarked. As you cross the field the tower of the church will be visible. Walk straight ahead alongside the hedge in the next field to the corner and clamber over a not very good piece of fencing and then walk to the gate just beyond. The gate opens outwards into the lane. Turn left in the lane and back to your car.

Historical Notes

The battle of Blore Heath: Blore Heath is a Wars of the Roses site. The houses of Lancaster and York, the red and white roses, were at war for many years before the House of Lancaster triumphed and Henry VII came to the throne in 1485. The battle of Blore Heath occurred on 23rd September 1459. The battle was centred along the steep banks of Hemp Mill Brook. The fight was between 5,000 Lancastrian troops sent out by Queen Margaret from Eccleshall Castle under the command of Lord Audley, and 10,000 Yorkist troops under the Earl of Salisbury who were en route from York to Ludlow. It was the Earl of Salisbury who, later that day, rode at the head of his troops into Market Drayton. Seeing the Yorkist centre retreat, Lord Audley had sent his foot soldiers forward, but it was a ruse and they were cut down by the Yorkist archers and the day was lost. Lord Audley was killed in action. Queen Margaret, who had witnessed the battle, fled after having the blacksmith reverse her horse's shoes in order to confuse her pursuers. The anvil on which this was done can still be seen at Mucklestone to the north of the A53 main road.

Market Drayton: Perhaps the most famous son of this town is Robert Clive, Clive of India, who as a child terrified the inhabitants of the town when he climbed the church tower and sat on one of the gargoyles. The boy went on to add India to the British Empire, 'the pearl in the crown'. Pitt's heaven-born general was a bit of a lad in those early days for it is said he ran what today we would call a 'protection racket' in that small sums of money were collected from shopkeepers in the town to ensure their windows did not get broken!

On 10th August 1651 most of the centre of the town was destroyed by fire and although public subscriptions raised money to alleviate the suffering most of it was misappropriated. This turned out to be a blessing in disguise, for the rebuilding was done in the original timber-framing and some examples still stand, among them the Crown Inn, the Sandbrook Vaults and the Star.

The Shropshire Union Canal was built by Thomas Telford – one cannot go far in Shropshire without meeting works of this energetic man. In 1856 it was open to Liverpool to take goods from the Midlands to the port and vice-versa. During its hey-day Market Drayton did a flourishing trade, mostly in corn and coal, and Pickford's was one of the principal companies to run freight barges 'to all parts of the Kingdom'. The canal declined with the coming of the railway, now itself closed, but in recent years increased leisure time has resulted in the resurrection of the canal for pleasure purposes.

The Four Alls – the nearest public house. The four 'Alls', as the sign outside shows, are

> (1) The king 'I rule all'
> (2) The bishop 'I pray for all'
> (3) The soldier 'I fight for all'
> (4) and the luckless citizen 'I pay for all!'

Bridgnorth
and The Severn Way

Introduction: The area around Bridgnorth is very agricultural, growing a variety of crops as well as dairy farming. The main walk takes in a pretty deciduous copse, a pine copse, a disused railway and a riverside walk. It's a very quiet walk through fields and over streams and mainly on the level. As the main walk is rather long a much shorter alternative is described, including a riverside section, and this could be included in a town walkabout as Bridgnorth is a very attractive town with plenty to see.

Distance: Long walk 7 miles (allow four hours). Short walk 3½ miles. Map — OS Landranger 138.

Refreshments: There are several inns and restaurants in Bridgnorth and at the Severn Valley railway station.

How to get there: Bridgnorth is situated 17 miles south-east of Shrewsbury and due west of Wolverhampton. It is easily accessible by road, the A458 from Shrewsbury, the A454 from Wolverhampton and the A442 from Telford. The walk starts from the car park in Whitburn Street, but can be adapted from any of the several car parks in the town. A nearby car park is signposted as short stay but both cost the same, or there is another at the fire station (marked F on the map) and behind the Severn Valley railway station. (GR 720922).

The Walk: Turn left from the car park along Whitburn Street towards the church. Turn left into High Street and pass under the North Gate.
The short walk: Keep along the road and fork right at the road junction ahead. Then turn right into Stanley Lane and walk along this, it is very quiet, passing the golf club until you arrive at the red-brick deserted farmhouse Little Severn Hall. Turn right on the track and go ahead across the railway track bed to the river. Turn right at the stile and return to Bridgnorth as described below.
The long walk: Take the high level path past the hospital and join Innage Lane by the fire station (F). Pass the school (S) and the Bridgnorth football ground. Turn right into Greenfields Road which drops down slightly and bears left. At the end turn right into Dingle View. At the end, by a house called The Woodlands there is a short flight of steps, at the bottom of which turn left along a well defined path between Dingle Woods and the houses. At a path junction bear half-left towards houses and an area of open ground. Keep alongside the hedge to rejoin the path again and drop down a slope (can be slippery) to a footbridge over the stream. Beyond it turn left uphill and along a level stretch

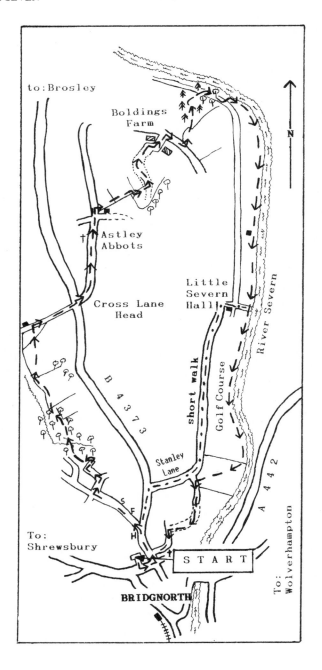

(also slippery). Where paths fork on the edge of a field go left down a short slope which then rises again and emerges over a waymarked stile into a large field.

The short stretch through Dingle Woods can be extremely slippery after rain and great care should be exercised; walking boots or strong walking shoes are advised. In wet weather, if in doubt, walk along the B4373 to Cross Lane Head, it is not busy and there is either a footpath or wide verge.

Keeping the hedge on your left go ahead to a double-stile linked by a plank bridge. Cross the next field half-right using the red-brick house as a guide. Cross the last triangular-shaped field and a narrow copse, and turn right at the lane.

At Cross Lane Head go directly over as signposted 'Astley Abbots ¼'. Pass right through the village to a crossroads (three roads and a track). Pass the gate house and immediately turn right over a waymarked stile and follow the path alongside a fence through two fields. Turn right over a stile and through a corner copse to a second stile just feet beyond. Turn left in a new large field, and keep alongside the hedge on the left to join a track coming from the right. This soon becomes well defined and passes through Boldings Farm yard; turn right then left, to emerge onto the lane beyond. Turn right.

One hundred yards along the lane, on a bend, by a small pull-in and a copse, turn left over a stile by a gate, and bear left around the field edge to another gate which leads into a pine copse. The track is well defined and drops downhill bearing right eventually to emerge onto the track bed of the former railway line from Shrewsbury to Bridgnorth. Turn right. In just a few yards pass between two gate posts. Here you have a choice of parallel paths, either turn left off the embankment along the edge of a field to the river and turn right or walk along the track-bed. The riverside fields are often growing crops, which might pose a problem in wet weather as the path is not cleared to the legal limit (1 metre) and as cereal crops retain the raindrops long after the rain has passed you can easily get wet through in less than no time, so, if you prefer, use the railway track-bed as an alternative. You pass a beautiful black and white farmhouse halfway along and on nearing Little Severn Hall (red brick) turn left at a crossroads of tracks from where you can now see the golf course. Turn right at the stile by the river.

(Short walk joins here.) The riverside path is easy to follow. As you approach Bridgnorth you will see why it was of such strategic importance to the Normans; the castle is now no longer visible, but if you can picture it in your mind using the church as an aid you will appreciate the importance of the site. Overlooking the river valley as it did, it also had a commanding view of the countryside around.

The unusual red-brick building the other side of the river is known as Fort Pendlestone. After passing the golf course you cross a side stream by a rather elaborate bridge to enter the public playing fields. Fork half-right towards the lamp-posts at the end of the houses. Turn left at the road. The road ends shortly, it's a cul-de-sac, but a paved footpath starts here and goes uphill past the scout hut. Turn left at the top and go straight ahead when the road turns right and in a few yards you will come to the church. Walk down the lane in front of the church and on regaining the High Street turn left under the town gate. On emerging the other side turn round to read the inscription over the archway. Turn right into Whitburn Street for the car park.

Historical Notes

Bridgnorth: There is a lot to see in Bridgnorth. The Northgate Museum is housed in the Burgess Hall of the North Gate above the road. The museum contains exhibits of local history. The Town Hall which dates from 1652 is one of the few remaining stilted town halls in Britain and contains a courtroom and council chamber. Another fine half-timbered building is the Swan Inn and the whole street is a delight to see, wide and elegant with the backdrop of the North Gate to set it off.

Bridgnorth is a two-tier town. The main town is set high above the river where we find the church and the castle, and Low Town is where once the river port was situated. The two are connected by the only inland cliff-railway in Britain, which was opened in 1892 when it was worked by water power. It was a busy river port until the mid 19th century and before that an important iron and carpet town. On the town side of the river it is still possible to see the old dock-side buildings and above them in the red sandstone cliffs the caves once used as houses and storage places. The precipitous Cartway, once the only way up for wheeled traffic, winds uphill right from the foot of the cliff-railway and walking up it we pass the 16th century house in which Bishop Percy was born and nearby the Prince Charles Inn. At the top we come to Castle Walk, described by Charles I as 'the finest in my dominion'. There were originally two castles and from here we look out over the valley where, beyond the railway station is Pampudding Hill, the location of the other castle of which no trace now remains.

During the Civil Wars Bridgnorth Castle held out for the King against Parliament and has the dubious honour of having had a personal visit from Cromwell, who oversaw the attack, his only authenticated visit to Shropshire and at which he was very nearly killed. Hearing that Charles I himself was about to arrive, Cromwell and his forces withdrew only to return later to resume the siege, which was met with determined resistance. Even the bombardment from point blank range of cannon situated on Pampudding Hill failed and the castle only fell after the Parliamentarians mined the foundations. Pampudding Hill is now the car park for the railway.

St Mary's church is in typical Telford style while outside some very fine Georgian houses set the seal to a very elegant part of the town.

It is fitting that the Severn Valley Railway should be housed here, one of Britain's longest preserved lines, as it was here in Bridgnorth in 1808 that Richard Trevithick built the world's first steam passenger locomotive.

Fort Pendlestone: The present building, built of rock hewn from the cliffs above it, replaced, in 1854, a 13th century cornmill given by Henry III to the inhabitants. There are caves in the cliff face above, which is 'High Rock'. There used to be a flat stone there called Taylor's Stone after a local tailor who said he would make a coat while sitting on it. Unfortunately, while engaged in this task he dropped his thimble and while stooping to retrieve it he lost his footing and fell to his death on the road below.

Hampton Loade and Highley

Introduction: A very pleasant and easy country walk, mostly on level ground. The walk goes south over high ground giving splendid views over the Severn Valley, and returns along the riverside Severn Way with the steam Severn Valley Railway alongside. The walk is very comfortably graded with only slight slopes at either end and for the most part well defined. The road walking is short and quiet.

Distance: 4 miles (allow two hours). Map — OS Landranger 138.

Refreshments: The King's Arms on the B4555 junction with the Hampton Loade lane, the Unicorn Inn at Hampton Loade, and light refreshments at Hampton Loade station.

How to get there: Hampton Loade is situated off the B4555 5 miles south of Bridgnorth. Leave Bridgnorth on the B4363 Cleobury Mortimer road, but fork left before the railway bridge onto the B4555 signposted Eardington and Highley. Two miles beyond Chelmarsh and just before The King's Arms turn sharp left as signposted 'Hampton Loade 1½ miles'. Park either at the station, small charge, or at the ferry, or at The Unicorn inn (but ask permission first). (GR 746865).

The Walk: Assuming you start from the station, turn left under the bridge and up the lane. When the lane turns sharp right, turn left by a bridleway sign onto a wide track. Pass through the farmyard by two facing gates and across a short field, a third facing gate gives entry to a wide grassy track hedged in on both sides. After a mile the track passes through a narrow copse to emerge into a field where it is less defined. Continue ahead with a hedge on the right through two fields. In the third field is a wide well defined track heading for the farm and a wide grassy area on your right.

The short cut: Continue ahead along a well defined track towards the farm, with a wire fence on your left, but when the fence ends fork left downhill across a large field. Go through the bridle gate at the bottom corner and cross the next field towards a cream coloured gate. Cross straight through the farmyard and go along the lane. Watch for a stile on your left. Turn left and crossing two fields, downhill, reach a small wood. Bear left and go down to the railway. After crossing turn left along a level track which soon drops down to the river's edge. Turn left, and follow the river back to Hampton Loade.

35

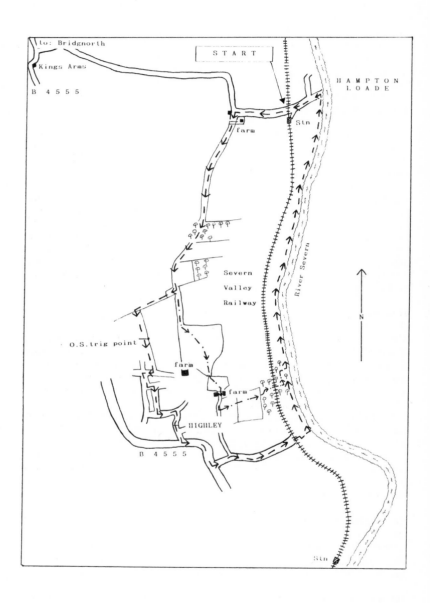

Turn right for the *main walk*. Go over the stile in the top corner and on breasting the hill you get a stupendous view westwards to the Clee Hills near Ludlow and a vast expanse of green fields.

By the wooden electricity pylon is a waymarked stile. Go over and walk straight ahead along the edge of the field, passing an Ordnance Survey triangulation point and arriving on the edge of Highley village. Turn right in the lane, Beech Street, turn left, and opposite No 46 turn left then almost immediately right onto a footpath between the houses. At the next road, turn left (no name) and in a few yards turn right into a short cul-de-sac. At the end a tarmac path begins between two facing houses, walk along this to the next road, this is the B4555 again. Turn left for about 100 yards and then take the first lane on the left, Vicarage Lane, with a 'No Through Road' sign. This lane shortly turns into a rough track and forking right by the camping site sign, gets narrower as it drops gently downhill to cross the railway.

You are welcomed to the Severn Valley Country Park by a plan of the area which shows, in large scale, many footpaths so if you wish to adapt the walk please do. If you wish to return to Hampton Loade by train, take the wide path right and at the Alveley Bridge turn right again uphill, then follow the path along the edge of the railway (take care when trains come) to the station, a walk of about ½ mile. Otherwise, cross the wide path and go down the flight of steps opposite to the river's edge and turn left along the river bank. It's a very pleasant level walk through grassy fields back to Hampton Loade and the start of the walk.

Historical Notes

The Severn Valley Railway was formed in 1853 and the line opened for normal traffic in 1862. It originally ran from Shrewsbury to Hartlebury, a distance of 40 miles, but now is not able to go further north than Bridgnorth. The company has, bit by bit, extended its operations from its original 'troncon' at Hampton Loade for a further 16 miles to its new terminus at Kidderminster where it links with the BR main line.

The line was closed during the Beeching era in 1963, the last passenger train running on 7th September. The line remained open for coal traffic until 1970 when the first section was bought for £25,000. On the 23rd May 1970 the first passenger train left Bridgnorth for Hampton Loade, the return fare, first class being nine shillings (45p). The line is now a major tourist attraction and the workshops at Bridgnorth are always extremely busy with restoration work, not only for the SVR, but for other preserved railways.

The Highley Mine opened in 1874 and produced good quality coal, hence the extensive sidings which have now been landscaped to form the Severn Valley Country Park. Notice that the ground is still black from coal dust even though the pit closed in 1969. Stone from the nearby quarries was floated downstream for the building of Worcester Cathedral. No trace of the mine remains.

Hampton Loade: The word 'Loade' is a Saxon word meaning 'ford', by which the residents of Highley and Chelmarsh formerly crossed to Quatt and Alveley.

A ferry has been working for over a century and the road by which you drove here, and the bridlepath which you walked were both once equally busy with local traffic using the ford to cross the river.

The ferry is quite an attraction in its own right with its unusual method of propulsion — river power! The ferryman by the delicate use of the rudder uses the current, which gives the propulsion, while an overhead cable guides it across. In 1964 a ferryman was drowned when the abnormally high tide swept the ferry away.

Highley has a population of over 3,000 and, with the recent modern housing developments, is now one of the largest villages in the county. Mentioned in the Domesday Book, it is named after the lord of the manor, Rudolf De Hugeli. On the main road one can still see the original miners' cottages typical of a mining area almost anywhere in Britain. The actual pit was situated at Alveley on the other side of the river.

Much Wenlock

Introduction: Who has not heard of Wenlock Edge, famed in word and song by the poems of A.E. Housman set to music by various composers including Ralph Vaughan-Williams. Much Wenlock is situated at the north-eastern end of the Edge in a hollow with low rolling hills around it on every side. It is not only in a delightful setting but is itself a delightful market town with many attractive buildings in the main streets. The view from the new gift-shopping precinct is especially delightful. The walk also takes in items of interest including, on the way out, the ancient abbey, the old railway station and part of the line, a former windmill and on the return a fine view over the whole town.

Distance: 5½ miles (allow two and a half hours). Map — OS Landranger 138.

Refreshments: Several inns in Much Wenlock.

How to get there: Much Wenlock is situated south-east of Shrewsbury on the A458 Bridgnorth road. Park in the main car park in St Mary's Street, which is parallel to High Street. From Shrewsbury, after passing abutments of the railway bridge on arriving at Wenlock, bear right by the Gaskell Arms Hotel onto the Bridgnorth road, and by the petrol station turn first left into St Mary's Street. The car park is next left. (GR 625000).

The Walk: In the far left-hand corner of the car park a cobbled way (bear right) leads to an archway and into a small and very attractive gift-shopping precinct from where there is a fine view along Wilmore Street. Walk along Wilmore Street past the church and turn first right for Wenlock Abbey.

Just before the abbey car park turn left through the wrought-iron kissing gate, just at the start of the pull-in, into a large field, and with your back to the road, go straight ahead up the field towards a line of trees. Notice the symmetrical edge to the lower branches of the trees, this is caused by animals grazing the lower leaves thus giving the trees that distinctive look.

Ahead of you now are what appear to be three stiles. Ignore the two on the right, they are private, go over the stile to the left and in doing so cross the track bed of the former GWR railway line and turn right in front of the very attractive former station. It is a perfect example of a beautifully restored rural station. Now used as a private dwelling, it has lost none of its former character with the railway offices at one end and the public waiting room at the other still apparent, and in summer the flower beds are a blaze of colour just as they

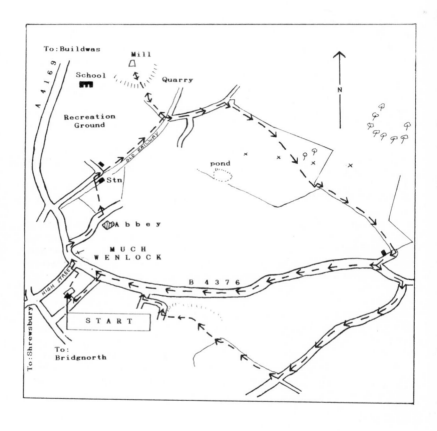

would have been in the days of the railway. Note also the fine tracery in wrought iron on the roof and the carvings in the stonework.

Now walk on straight ahead through what at first look like level-crossing gates, which give onto a level path alongside the park and recreation ground. The old track bed is on the right and can be walked if you wish. Continue along this path and after passing through another kissing gate at the end, turn left for a short distance on a dirt track and through another gate and thence to an open grassy hill. On climbing the hill you will come to the former windmill now devoid of sails but giving a good view of the town and countryside around.

You now retrace your steps back to the park gate, but bear left on a narrow path between the bushes and trees and cross the railway track bed by two short flights of steps on either side. Go ahead to a narrow lane and turn left as far as the entrance gate to Downsmill. Here turn right. There is a stile, but the cross plank is broken, so use the gate and go into a field, crossing a stream by a little humped bridge. Turn left after the bridge alongside the hedge (with a disused waymarked stile at the corner). Follow this hedge up the field until you see in front of you two wooden electricity pylons. The path crosses the field midway between them to a wooden fence beyond. At the corner of the field is a waymarked stile.

Go over the stile and turn right in the new field, keeping alongside the hedge, now on the right, and continue to the end of the field where a field gate leads into a rough lane. Turn right towards the house and so to the road. This is only a minor B class road with not much traffic but it is fast moving so great care is advised. To shorten the walk, turn right and follow the road back to Much Wenlock.

To continue on the main walk, turn left up the hill as far as the first turning right (no signpost) into a quiet lane. Walk along this until you come over the brow of the hill with fine views westwards to the Clee Hills above Ludlow; you will see the transmitter on the top. Just after the word 'slow' painted on the road there is an entrance to a farm (left) with black barns; opposite this track on the other side of the road is a field gate. Turn right here, through the gate, and follow the path alongside the hedge, on the right, to a stile at the end of the field. Go over and bear slightly left across a rough grassy field. From here there is a very good view over the town with the windmill beyond it, and if you have sharp eyes, you can just see the tip of a gable-end of the abbey peeping over the tree-tops. The not indistinct path rounds the hill and drops gently down to a stile between bungalows partially hidden by the hedge and trees. On reaching the road, turn right downhill, and you rejoin the B4376 to turn left into Much Wenlock.

Historical Notes

Wenlock Abbey: From AD 625 to AD 655 Penda was King of Mercia, Mercia being the Kingdom of the Midlands stretching from East Anglia to the Severn. It was later extended westwards to the Welsh border by King Offa. Penda was a pagan king but his grand-daughter was Christian and it was she who in the 7th century became the first abbess of Wenlock Abbey either at or shortly after its founding in AD 690. After being destroyed by the Danes it was restored by a certain Lady Godiva. Destroyed again after the Conquest, it was soon restored by the Norman baron Roger de Montgomery who found St Milburga's tomb during the rebuilding of the church. Mercia became Christian in AD 655 when Penda was slain in battle and his son Merewalh became king. Many legends surround the saint's name, including several wells with healing properties. Wenlock owes its main claim to fame to the abbey. It is beautifully situated and must have been a most impressive building in its prime, its church alone was of cathedral size. The only pre-Conquest religious house in Shropshire, the abbey was for a time a double monastery, that is to say, it had both nuns and brothers but it is evident they kept themselves to themselves as each had their own church. The male community may have had a continuous existence until the dissolution by Henry VIII.

Much Wenlock was once a thriving centre for leathercraft, wheelwrighting and brewing and many aspects of these bygone trades and others are exhibited in the museum at the corner of High Street and Barrow Street. The town lost its importance with the rise of Ironbridge during the Industrial Revolution.

The Guildhall rests on the stout oak arches of the butter market, and iron rings on one of the pillars suggest it was once used as a whipping post. It is a most eye-catching half-timbered building constructed in just two days in 1577. The panelled court room and council chambers are upstairs and open to the public and here are kept the old stocks made for three persons, unique in being fitted with wheels so that they could be moved around the town for the benefit of public enjoyment!

The railway was part of the GWR empire. The line starting at Wellington went through Wenlock to join the Shrewsbury – Hereford line near Craven Arms, but only three trains a day made the complete journey, though there was an intensive service from Wenlock to Wellington. The journey was a very leisurely affair taking 15 minutes for the 3 miles from Wenlock to Buildwas! The line lasted just 100 years, opening in 1862 and closing in 1962.

Ironbridge Gorge

Introduction: Little did Abraham Darby realise when he mastered a way to smelt iron with coke just what it would lead to, the start of the greatest Industrial Revolution this nation has ever seen. Now the furnaces are cold and the smoke and belching flames doused for ever. Almost literally from the ashes has arisen along the most beautiful stretch of the river Severn the Ironbridge Museum, now recognised as a World Heritage Site and containing no less than eight different museum sites. Denoted as 'M1', etc on the map, each is devoted to a different aspect of the Gorge's former greatness. Now we can walk the many footpaths and enjoy the unrivalled scenery of the Gorge, which with the museums is the Gorge's present claim to fame. The walk traverses both banks of the river and apart from a short climb at the start is level all the way and gives superb views first of one bank and then the other. It might even be classified as 'a pub crawl walk' for there are no less than seven public houses en route!

Distance: 4 miles (allow three hours, excluding stops and museum visits). Map — OS Landranger 138.

Refreshments: There is the Railway Hotel by the car park at the start and a further six public houses and two cafés along the way. There are several restaurants in Ironbridge.

How to get there: Ironbridge is situated south-east of Shrewsbury, between Shrewsbury and Bridgnorth. From Shrewsbury take the A458 Kidderminster road as far as Much Wenlock. On entering Wenlock, turn left opposite the Gaskell Arms onto the A4169 signed Buildwas Abbey. Over the bridge at Buildwas, turn right for Ironbridge B4373. Drive through Ironbridge and beyond the chemist's shop, fork right signposted Broseley. Turn right at the traffic lights, signposted The Iron Bridge (P), over a narrow bridge, then right again and at the hairpin bend go straight ahead to the car park opposite the Railway Hotel. (GR 672003).

The Walk: The car park is built on the site of the former Ironbridge railway station and if you look to the left as you leave by a narrow exit, you will see the rails still embedded in the road surface. Turn right over the Iron Bridge (M1) where there is a converted toll house now used as an information centre. There is a splendid view both ways from the bridge, up and down stream, but better views of the bridge, for the photographer, can be had from the public viewpoints, to left and right, on the town side. Upstream, to your left, from

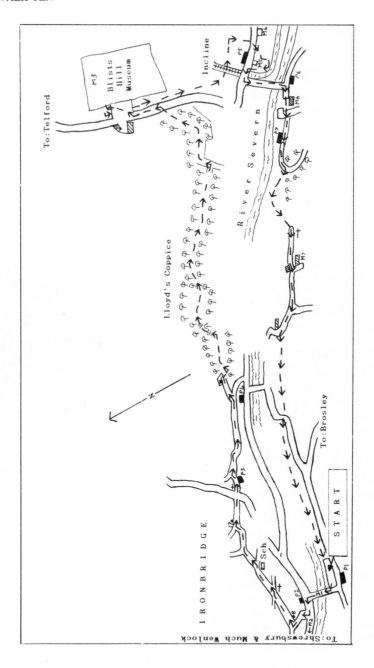

the bridge you can see one of the museums. The Museum of the River (M2) is also a Visitors Centre with video films etc, and worth a visit if you have time. From the bridge note the church as you pass this on the walk.

Cross the road and opposite the Tontine Inn (pub 2) turn left. Turn right up Severn Bank with a gift shop on the corner. (The main information centre is a few yards further along the main road.) At the top of the bank, opposite No 14 turn right passing No 8 Bath Road. From time to time you will get entrancing views over the town and down to the iron bridge below. Cross over bisecting roads by St Luke's church and into St Luke's Road, still going uphill. By the former school fork left, again uphill, in a narrow lane. At the top of the hill, where a red brick wall ends and a low stone wall begins, go ahead on the level (at last). Opposite No 17 by a GR letter box in the wall on your right, turn right.

Cross the main road and head for The Golden Ball (pub 3). Make use of the mirror on the facing lamp-post to see round the sharp corner to the right. The church is now converted into dwellings. Passing the inn continue ahead, skirting its car park. Dropping downhill, pass Honeysuckle Cottage 44 and after passing the last cottage there is an embankment on the left (if you need refreshment now, continue along the lane to the road then turn right, there is an inn (pub 4).

Opposite a street lamp fixed to telephone post No 47710, fork left onto a rough track going uphill. Pass in front of a cottage and before the wicket gate into the garden, turn hard right onto an overgrown track alongside the fence (on your left). In just a few yards through the trees turn left up a short slope towards a wooden electricity pylon and there you will find the path opens out into a wide clearing with patches of heather. Go straight ahead and at the third pylon and in sight of the road below, turn left into woods and a flight of wooden steps. Ignoring the level path on the left halfway up, bear right to a second flight of steps and later bear left to a third and a fourth flight which brings you to a second clearing with patches of heather. A notice board telling you about coppicing will confirm you are on the route. Bear right across the clearing to find a well defined path in the far corner which soon skirts an overgrown pond choked with bullrushes. The path is now easy to follow with several short flights of steps here and there until eventually you come to a T junction opposite a field. Turn left up a short hill where shortly you will pass two former charcoal kilns and examples of the original and finished products. A wide track now leads you out of the wood, passing former brick kilns (on left) onto the main road. Turn left along the road for 200 yards.

At the private car park opposite Hillcrest, bear half-right towards the far right-hand corner. A path drops gently down to join another path. Turn left into the tunnel (if you wish to visit the Blists Hill museum turn right). You are now walking along the Silkin Way, a former railway line. After 15 minutes you come to the famous Great Hay Incline bridge (more about this later). Continue a little further until you come to a unique signpost, the wheel of a railway locomotive, set in concrete. Now turn right down a flight of steps to a large car park and picnic area by the Shakespeare Inn (pub 5). Cross the road to a wooden field gate nearly opposite with a nice grassy bank for picnics and rests. Bear right on a rough track which bends left to the canal then back right again to a café and entrance to The Tar Tunnel. Go up steps and turn left over the bridge (narrow). This is the end of the canal and from the bridge is a very good view of the Great Hay Incline with its railway still in place, the subject of many a photograph and picture postcard.

Now turn left, signed Severn Valley Way, and dropping down the other side of the canal basin cross the river by a footbridge to the Boat Inn (pub 6). Turn right along Ferry Road which soon becomes a path behind the Jackfield Mill, Maws Craft Centre and Dancing Clows Café. Cross straight over onto a tarmac path to reach the Half Moon Inn (pub 7). Follow the approach road to a hair-pin bend, where you turn right by a short post painted in red and white bands. A rough path now dips down to the river then left up towards the church where you join a proper road. Continue ahead by Crossing Cottage opposite the entrance to the Jackfield Tile Museum. A footpath, using the track bed of the former Shrewsbury-Bridgnorth railway begins just beyond the Chapel Lane street sign (note the original level crossing gates still in place). The path is now easy to follow and brings you right back to the car and the Railway Hotel (pub 1).

Historical Notes

Ironbridge Gorge, now a designated World Heritage Centre, was the birthplace of the Industrial Revolution. The wealth of attractions with its eight museums and delightful scenery make it a place to pass several days. The museums offer exceptional value in that by buying a Passport Ticket you pay to visit all the museums but in your own time, in any order and you do not have to do them all in one day as the ticket is not limited in time.

It was here that in 1709 the Quaker Abraham Darby perfected his technique to smelt iron using coke and thus was born the Coalbrookdale Company. At the time iron was smelted by using charcoal but it was in short supply and the Darby innovation enabled cheap iron to be made by mass production for the first time. The Iron Bridge, the first such bridge in the world, was a later addition, being built by his grandson, also Abraham, in 1779. Three hundred and eight tons of iron went into its construction. It was closed to vehicular traffic in 1934. The choice of Ironbridge was a result of the abundance in one place of coal, iron, transport and water power. Since the demise of the industrial activities the valley has been undisturbed and regained its former charm and greenery.

The Museums: Each is devoted to a different aspect of the industrial life of the Gorge, and a fully detailed illustrated leaflet is available from the Toll House or information centre. The Museum of the River (M2) includes a 40 ft model of how the Gorge looked in 1796. Blists Hill (M3) is the largest of the museums and the first to be opened. It covers 50 acres and is a step back in time to the Victorian era, even to the extent of using Victorian money. It is a fully working museum with a pub, candle factory, and a butcher making real pies. Hot meals and snacks are available and the museum's brochure says to allow at least two and a half hours, but I think this is on the conservative side. Beneath Blists Hill is the Tar Tunnel which takes you underground to see the bitumen oozing from the walls. Nearby is the Coalport China Museum.

The Great Hay Incline lifted barges from the lower basin of the Shropshire Canal by the Tar Tunnel, to the upper section by Blists Hill Museum.

The Silkin Way: A former LMS railway line, which ran from Coalport north through what is now Telford, to join the LMS line from Wellington to Stafford. The main Severn Valley line on the other side of the river was owned by the GWR. The Silkin Way is named after the Labour MP Lewis (later Lord) Silkin, who was responsible in the Labour Government of 1945-50 for the New Towns Act of 1946, the Town and Country Planning Act 1947 and the National Parks Act of 1949. The way which runs from Coalport Wharf to Wellington was opened in 1977 by the then Prime Minister, James Callaghan.

The footbridge over the river between the Shakespeare Inn and the Boat Inn was built in 1921 and is unique in being also the war memorial. Read the plaque at the start of the bridge which gives the history of it; in the centre is another plaque with the names of those who gave their lives.

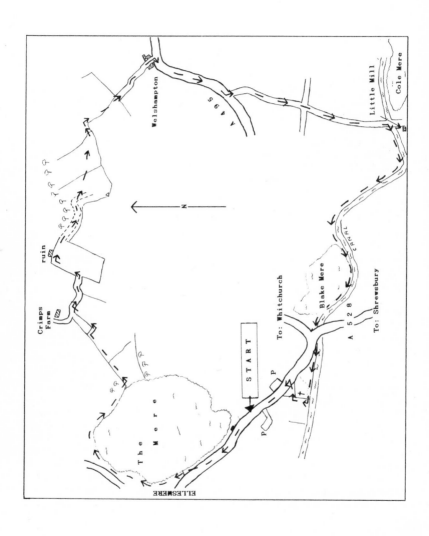

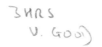

WALK ELEVEN

The Lakes of Ellesmere

Introduction: The Shropshire Plain stretches north from Shrewsbury to merge with Cheshire, and in the north-west corner of the county is Shropshire's Lake District. There are ten large lakes and many small lakes. The largest of these is The Mere at Ellesmere on which this walk is founded. Set among gently rolling fields and coppices it is a delightfully easy place for a walk, level and quiet yet always with something to attract and interest. The meres themselves are a hive of activity for the wildfowl which inhabit them and all manner of bird life which lives along the shores. Ellesmere itself is a quiet rural town with some attractive buildings.

Distance: 5 miles (allow three and a half hours). Map — OS Landranger 126.

Refreshments: At the start is The Boat House and conveniently situated at the halfway stage the Sun Inn at Welshampton. Numerous other inns and cafés in Ellesmere.

How to get there: Ellesmere is 17 miles north-west of Shrewsbury on the A528 road. There are many parking places on either side of the approach road. (GR 400950).

The Walk: Walk along the lake side towards the town and bear right to the water's edge when you see the sign 'Bird feeding area'. Go through the kissing gate between the road and the lake into the town's gardens, and follow the path through a very pleasant lakeside park. The gardens and the lake were given to the Shropshire County Council by the 6th Baron Brownlow in 1953 to be kept as a public amenity. The path continues well beyond the formal gardens into a wilder area but still alongside the lake. On leaving the trees turn left into a grassy field (the stile is waymarked). Walk away from the lake up an easy slope alongside the hedge (on your left). Go straight ahead at the next waymarked stile, still alongside the hedge and skirting round the newly planted copse come eventually to Crimps Farm, an elegant three storey building. Turn right at the lane, as signposted by the public footpath sign and follow the track until it peters out in a field. Turn left towards the next building, the chimney of which can be seen over the rise. The cottage is derelict. Just beyond it continue ahead by way of another waymarked stile, but don't miss the view behind you. From here, although the ground is a mere 300 ft above sea level, the view across the Shropshire Plain to the Welsh Mountains is one not to be missed.

Continue along the wide well defined track into the next field. When the track turns right uphill by a circular water trough (there is an OS triangulation point on the brow) bear slightly left, keeping more or less in a straight line with the track you were on, and immediately ahead of you to the east, you will see a stile. Go up that field to the far left-hand corner by the copse, the stile is not visible until you get to it. Go through and follow the hedge, on the right, which shortly makes a sharp right-hand turn. Skirting a pond go straight ahead to join a farm lane which brings you to the main road on the outskirts of Welshampton.

To get to the inn in the middle of the village, turn left, otherwise turn right along the A495 for ¼ mile. Do take great care, it is a busy road. Turn left at the first lane on the left with the sign 'Unsuitable for motor vehicles' and follow this to the canal, going straight ahead at the intervening crossroads. On reaching the canal at Little Mill, turn right along the towpath and follow this back to Ellesmere.

On the way you pass Blake Mere on the right with its welcoming signs of 'Do Nots'! The canal then burrows under the Shrewsbury road by way of a tunnel beyond which, on your right, is a way up to the road. Ignore it. Continue along by the tranquil waters until you pass the Roman Catholic convent complex on your right. It is a large grey stone building surrounded by a high wooden fence sometimes clothed in ivy, and where the fence ends there is a stile into a field. Go up the field, away from the canal, to a second stile at a right-hand turning and cross the next field still alongside the hedge, heading for a double poled electricity pylon sporting a transformer. Cross the road beyond and turn left back to the car.

Historical Notes

The Meres: Unlike the great lakes of the Lake District, the lakes here are not fed by streams or rivers from the surrounding countryside. The water level is maintained by seepage through the surrounding soil and the level of the water relates to the water table in the surrounding area. Draining as it does the surrounding area, this water is very rich in nutrients which encourages a wide variety of animal and plant life. Thus in a very dry summer, when the surrounding area would be unusually dry, the water level would fall in concert. The Mere at Ellesmere, the largest of the meres, covers an area of 116 acres and is 60 ft deep at its deepest point. The word 'mere' is of Anglo-Saxon origin meaning 'lake'. The meres were formed by the remains of the melting glaciers some 12,000 years ago. Bream, perch and pike are fished from the waters, and their importance in former days was underlined when a Bronze Age canoe was dug out.

The Meres Visitor Centre and Watch Centre are well worth a visit. The latter includes various live animal displays including small mammals, amphibians and pond life and is a great way to introduce young children to the wonder of nature.

Colemere is the second largest of the lakes and is now a country park. You can visit it on the walk by continuing a few yards beyond the canal bridge at Little Mill and turning left at the first gate. A level path does a circuit of the lake. Or you can drive there, it is signposted off the A528 Shrewsbury road, to make a separate walk.

The canal was built in 1793 at a cost of £1,000,000. It eventually ran from the Llangollen Falls to the west as far as Hurleston Junction near Nantwich. Abandoned during the Second World War as a commercial institution, the canal is now seeing a new lease of life as a medium for inland pleasureboat holiday cruises. The old wharf is still in place together with its crane while the wharf buildings have been converted into craft industries. The tunnel is 87 yards long and one of the earliest canal tunnels to have a towpath. I need hardly mention the name of the engineer in charge of the canal construction, yes Thomas Telford (I wonder he ever found time to sleep!).

Ellesmere is a small market town dating back to Saxon times. The parish church of St Mary the Virgin is a landmark for miles around, and has a particularly fine peal of bells. Market days are Tuesdays and Fridays at the Market Hall in Scotland Street. Besides the canal, which was the first industrial incursion to bring importance to the town, the arrival of the railway added to Ellesmere's importance. This was no branch line but the main line of the Cambrian Railway from Aberystwyth. All trains from London came this way after reversing at Crewe. London trains were, however, not the main users, for the line's most popular run was to and from Manchester with which, via Crewe, it had a direct link. The old railway station, Cambrian House, an impressive building built as the head office of the Oswestry, Ellesmere and Whitchurch railway (which operated for the staggering time of two entire days before being absorbed by the Cambrian) is still preserved. The lines opened in 1864 and closed in 1965.

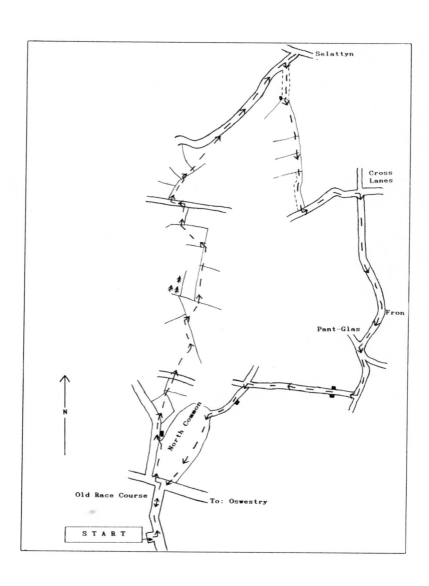

Oswestry Race Course

Introduction: In the north-west part of Shropshire, between the busy A5 trunk road and the Welsh Border is an area of Shropshire entirely by-passed by the 20th century rush. Here one can stroll, linger and drink in the fine views unhindered by traffic; an area of lanes which seem to lead nowhere in particular and do not seem in a hurry to get there. Oswestry race course, crossed by Offa's Dyke, closed in 1848. It is now common land, offering views across to the mountain ranges of Wales.

Distance: 5 miles (allow three hours). Map — OS Landranger 126.

Refreshments: The Cross Keys at Selattyn serves only liquid refreshments and is alongside the village shop where sweets and chocolates can be obtained. Several inns and cafés in Oswestry.

How to get there: Approaching Oswestry by car on the A5 from Shrewsbury, go straight ahead at the roundabout on the approach to Oswestry. Cross the railway bridge, and then fork left noting the sign to Selattyn — keep this in mind. At the traffic lights go straight ahead and take the first right, by a high red brick wall. This road, Welsh Walls, skirts round the back of the church and the park. At the 'stop' sign at the next junction turn left still signed Selattyn and then, by the fire station, fork left, as signposted with the brown sign 'Old Race Course'. At the top of the hill, turn left for ¼ mile to the visitors car park. (GR 258305).

The Walk: There is a large map of the area in the car park with many other walks shown which you may care to use another time. Just close by there is also a topograph.

Turn left out of the car park back the way you came as far as the T junction. Cross over but ignore the gravel track directly in front and also the first grassy track to its left, use instead the second grassy track alongside the road. A short road walk is necessary when you reach the stone house. About 150 yards beyond there is a lay-by on the right-hand side of the road; just beyond this, no more than a few feet, is a stile the other side of a shallow ditch.

Cross the stile and strike out, half-left, across the field to the far left-hand corner. Go over the stile there and the next stile immediately beyond to cross a third field to a lane. Cross the lane to a facing stile.

The next field is large and rather humpy. Head for the hump with the large rock on top, there is no clear path. However, once over the hump descend to the lower ground where a clear grassy path, parallel to the fence and assorted gorse bushes, runs to your left towards a conifer plantation.

Nearing the corner of the field find the stile on your right-hand side, cross it and turn half-left towards the next stile which is mid-way along the row of short trees which marks the field boundary. Continue ahead over the stile with a row of tall pine trees, later beeches, overhead and the conifer plantation across the field to your left. Continue downhill at the next stile into a valley but only as far as the first field gate on your left, by which is a stile. Cross the stile and go half-right down the side of a sloping field to find a rather concealed stile in the bottom, near a large boulder. Go over this stile and straight up the next field, hedge on right, to emerge onto a narrow lane. Turn left.

In just 5 yards, not more, look for a new stile on the other side of the lane. It is on the top of a short grassy bank. Go over and go up the field (hedge on left, with a grey stone cottage beyond). You pass two fields on your left and a field gate before coming to the next stile. Go over and turn sharp right to another stile just ahead. Over that and head towards the lane and a stile at the foot of the slope. Turn right along the lane to Selattyn. There are seats under the lychgate into the churchyard if you brought sandwiches.

For the return walk retrace your steps from the inn and turn right as signposted 'Old Race Course'. Just past the last cottage on the left is an old cart track. Follow this until it terminates by a derelict cottage. Go over the waymarked stile and turn left alongside the hedge. Continue ahead now through three facing field gates, with lovely views to your left, into a grassy lane which ends at a narrow road. Turn left.

Turn right at Cross Lanes crossroads as signposted 'Pant Glas'. The walk is on the lane now but it is very quiet with hardly any traffic at all and gives superb views across the Shropshire Plain to the east.

At the T junction by a telephone box, turn left and then bear right up the hill into the woods. At the top of the hill, turn right, with a field on your left and the woods on your right, onto a rough track which passes between the farm outbuildings and climbs a short hill. The track soon becomes a metalled lane again and at a crossroads with the name Rhosfach on your right, turn left onto a stony track. This track goes gently uphill to pass a cottage and emerges onto the north-east corner of North Common. Follow a well defined and wide grassy track back to the T junction and so back to your car.

Historical Notes

Oswestry Race Course: Closed in 1848 and now common land owned and managed by Oswestry Council. There are ample parking places, picnic tables and toilets. Offa's Dyke is, from the car park, to the west, the side farthest from the road. The area of the course is quite extensive, including North Common where the wide grassy track used on the outward and homeward legs of the walk follows the actual race track. There are extensive views from the west side of the Old Race Course too, right across the mountain ranges of Wales.

Oswestry is a bustling market town and former headquarters of the extensive Cambrian Railway. Oswestry however, dates back far beyond the railway era for on the northern outskirts of the town can be found the Old Oswestry hill fort, an extensive area of 15 acres of grassland surrounded by deep defensive banks and ditches making the whole area around 60 acres. The original Iron Age construction dates from around 600 BC. In Arthur Street is the Oswestry Cycle Museum and next door the headquarters of the present Cambrian Railway Preservation Society which plans to re-open the line to passengers from here to Gobowen on the BR Shrewsbury to Chester line. The old castle motte is still preserved and accessible from near the Guildhall.

The town is rich in history, being fought over many times. At first it was the English versus the Welsh as to whether the town was in England or Wales. The dispute was settled by the act of union in 1535 which planted it firmly in England, but Welsh is still freely spoken by many of the local people. In 1559 the plague killed off a third of the people and the Weeping Stone in Morda Street is a memorial to the disaster. The church is dedicated to St Oswald, from whom the town gets its name. After being captured by the pagan Saxon King of Mercia, Penda, Oswald was nailed alive to a tree, hence the name 'Oswald's tree'.

The poet Wilfred Owen was born in Oswestry in 1893 the son of a railway worker and might well have become one of our leading poets had he not been tragically killed by a stray bullet just a week before the Armistice in 1918, when he was 25 years old. The news of his death reached Oswestry the day the Armistice was declared. The town's war memorials consist of the pillars which form the entrance gates to the town park. Another famous son of Oswestry is the composer Henry Walford Davies, composer of 'Solemn Melody' and 'The March Past of the Royal Air Force'. In 1934 he succeeded Sir Edward Elgar as Master of the King's Musick. He died in 1941.

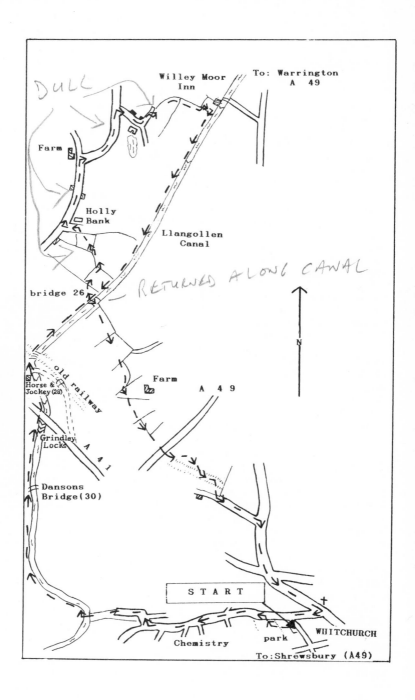

Whitchurch and The Llangollen Canal

Introduction: An easy level walk along the Shropshire/Cheshire border through some fine agricultural country and following the Llangollen Canal, with some interesting features such as the swing bridge at New Mills and the flight of locks at Grindley Brook which can afford much entertainment on a busy day. Wide views are enjoyed on every side as the canal is usually well above the surrounding countryside, which is rich and interesting.

Distance: 6 miles (allow four hours). Map — OS Landranger 117.

Refreshments: The village store at Grindley Locks, the Horse and Jockey at Bridge 28, the Willey Moor Inn, and several inns and cafés in Whitchurch.

How to get there: Whitchurch lies on the A49 Shrewsbury to Warrington road, due north of Shrewsbury. From Shrewsbury take the A49 as signposted Whitchurch. Go into the town and turn left on a right-hand bend into the town centre. Go straight over at the crossroads at the bottom of the hill into Castle Hill and the car park is on your left at the top. There is also a good railway service from Crewe and Shrewsbury and trains are nicely spaced to give time for a walk. (GR 512417).

The Walk: Leave the car park by a flight of steps into the Victoria Jubilee Park. Pass the bandstand and toilets and turn right along a tarmac path. As you pass a flight of steps to your right, notice the stone bridge. This marks the former end of the Whitchurch branch of the Llangollen Canal along the bed of which you will shortly be walking. Turn left along Smallbrook Road, later becoming Chemistry Road for about ½ mile until on a gentle left-hand curve you come to Bathfield Crescent (not named). There is a house opposite you the upper storey of which is half-timbered. Cross the road to a rough track crossing what, from here, appears to be a railway bridge. Walk down this track and you will find a public footpath sign on the right by the bridge. The bridge is not a railway bridge but crosses the former canal. After you turn left along a metalled stretch of the track, the canal bed can be seen below you to your left and when the metalled track ends, continue ahead actually walking along the old canal bed. Cross the canal by the New Mills bridge and turn right along the far side and continue to Grindley Locks.
    Descend the slope by the locks but do not cross the main road; opposite the shop a narrow concrete path drops steeply down and under the road alongside

the canal. There are three locks in this steep climb and a further three before you reach bridge 28. The track to the left leads to the Horse and Jockey and to the right it leads back to Whitchurch (via the A41 road) for those wishing to shorten the walk. From bridge 28 notice the tunnel ahead and another bridge to your right and between them the embankment of the former Whitchurch-Chester railway.

Continue along the tow path through the tunnel as far as bridge 26. The main walk now makes a loop which returns here and thus presents a further opportunity to make a short cut if desired.

Turn left as signposted 'Tushingham A41' and cross the stile. Fork right across the field. There are two stiles in the facing hedgerow (both waymarked), go over the stile to the right. It is not so noticeable as the other but beyond it is a wooden footbridge. Walk ahead now, with a hedge on the left towards a field gate dead ahead. Over the next waymarked stile walk up a gentle slope and notice what appears to be an ancient track the other side of the hedge; halfway up the field is another stile, turn left over it and the footbridge, and turn right again. At the top there is another stile in the corner near the red-brick house Holly Bank. Turn left onto a rough track and right into the lane.

Walk along a very quiet lane for ½ mile and take the first turning on the right, another metalled lane which drops downhill, passing an old lodge gate and with glimpses of Tushingham Hall, through a deep gully to emerge on level ground at a T junction with another track. Turn right here as signposted 'Sandstone Trail'. Pass the outbuildings and at a fork of lanes by a bungalow, turn left (as waymarked) towards a facing gate. Just before the gate turn right over a stile into a big field, and turn left (with a hedge on the left). Follow the hedge into the farthest corner of the field where there are two stiles one beyond the other. The white building ahead is the Willey Moor Inn and the way is well marked. On arriving at the canal turn right back to bridge 26 to complete the loop. It takes about an hour (not including any stops) to walk the loop.

Cross bridge 26 as signposted and go straight up the field towards the 'hump'. In the corner is what at first looks like a double archway and a stile is under the left arch. Continue ahead round the hump to the next stile. Go over that into the field beyond and skirting the field find a further stile on your left at 200 yards. Cross it and a bridge made of old sleepers, and fork right to a nearby stile. Continue ahead across the next field, using the wooden electricity pylon on the left as a guide, and dead ahead of it is a further stile partially concealed by a holly bush and also approached by a sleeper bridge. Go straight ahead again to a stile in the corner of the field at the end of what appears to be an embankment. Straight ahead again to the next stile by a wooden electricity pylon where the hedge (on left) ends. Cross the A49 road (take care) to a stile opposite and bear left along the hedgerow.

The embankment of the former Whitchurch-Chester line is now on your right and you soon come to another stile with no fence round it. Drop down and cross the stream by a sleeper bridge and another stile into a narrow field and forking gently left find another stile which brings you onto the railway track bed. Turn left along the track until near to houses, where you turn right through the fence and follow a well worn path across the field to a lane. Turn left along the lane and at the main road turn right for Whitchurch. Head for the church and by the Greyhound Inn turn right into Yardington. The car park is at the end of this street.

Historical Notes

Whitchurch owes its importance to being strategically placed across the main north-south route and the east-west route. Being placed on high ground it controlled not only these important routes but from its vantage point amid the Shropshire and Cheshire Plains, commanded the surrounding area. It was thus of great importance to the Romans and the Normans.

Whitchurch is Shropshire's most northerly town, right on the Cheshire border. It was built on the site of a Roman settlement. Mediolanum, as it was called, was mid-way between the two large Roman cities of Viroconium (near Shrewsbury) and Chester. No traces of the Roman town remain, but excavations during rebuilding have unearthed many artefacts.

The town was later settled by the Normans who built a fine white church which, in French, they called 'Blancminster'. This translated into early English as 'Whitechirche', and this later devolved into Whitchurch. The tall tower of St Alkmund's church dominates the town and the church is the largest 8th century church in the county outside Shrewsbury. Within its keeping is a memorial plaque to Edward German and the tomb of John Talbot. John Talbot was the first Earl of Shrewsbury. Born in Whitchurch he was later known as the 'Scourge of France' during his military exploits there during the Hundred Years War. In 'Henry VI part I' Shakespeare writes, 'The scourge of France, the Talbot so much feared that with his name mothers stilled their babies'. He was killed in action near Bordeaux in 1453, aged 80! His dying wish was that if slain abroad his heart was to be brought back to Whitchurch. This was done and it is buried under the porch at the church. It was a century later that his body was brought back and buried in the tomb by an ancestor. In 1711 the tower of the original 'white church' collapsed and in 1714 the present building was completed.

Although in Shropshire, the town is, paradoxically, the centre of the Cheshire cheese industry. Many locally made farmhouse cheeses, such as Shropshire Blue, can be sampled and bought at the Friday market.

Like Oswestry, Whitchurch also gave birth to a national composer, Sir Edward German. Born Edward German Jones in 1862 at a house in St Mary's Street, now the Back Street Vaults, he dropped the last part of his name and came to fame when asked by Richard D'Oyly Carte to complete an unfinished opera left by Sir Arthur Sullivan on his death. So popular was German's effort that he was commissioned to write more and his next and most famous work was 'Merrie England', first performed in 1902. He also wrote an opera based on Fielding's book 'Tom Jones', several symphonies and other works. He died in 1936 and is buried in the cemetery.

Grindley Locks: This portion of the Shropshire Union Canal is noted for the famous flight of six picturesque locks at Grindley, a local attraction for people who like to watch the boats slowly climbing up or down on their way to and from Wales. This is a very busy place in summer especially with 'gongoozlers' (the boatman's name for spectators). It can be quite an entertainment, especially with novices trying to work the locks correctly!

New Mills Bridge: The unusual type of bridge, known as a lift bridge, is one of three on the Llangollen Canal where a crossing was necessary but where clearance was insufficient for the construction of a conventional bridge. The mechanism is hydraulically operated, controlled by a windlass to prevent it dropping prematurely onto a passing boat.

The Sandstone Trail is a medium distance footpath created by the Cheshire County Council, and this walk uses part of it as it forms the towpath of the canal north of Whitchurch.

WALK FOURTEEN

Brown Clee

Introduction: Of the two Clee Hills, Brown Clee is the most attractive. Relatively unscathed by comparison with its neighbour Titterstone Clee, Brown Clee is an island hill surrounded by a low-lying agricultural area and offers some superb views and fine walks. On your walk you will come across real coal seams and an ancient British fort. Brown Clee is, south of the Pennines, the highest summit in England.

Distance: 6 miles. The outward leg is uphill and steep in places, but not difficult. Map — OS Landranger 137.

Refreshments: Various in Ludlow. None in the immediate vicinity but come prepared and enjoy a picnic in a beautiful setting.

How to get there: Brown Clee is 6 miles north-east of Ludlow. Leave Ludlow by the A4117 signed 'Clee Hill & Cleobury Mortimer'. Go straight ahead at the first roundabout on the A49 by-pass and a mile farther on turn left again signed 'B4364 Bridgnorth'. Three miles further turn left again signed Stoke St Milborough, passing St Millburga's well, and continue through that village for Clee St Margaret. One and a half miles from Stoke St Milborough you will, on a left-hand bend, come to open hillside (on your right) fenced off from the road, with a field gate directly in front of you and a parking space to one side with a lay-by. You can park here, or drive through, and park and picnic inside. (GR 569838).

The Walk: There are, at the start, many grassy tracks, choose any parallel to the hedge on the right. From here you can already see the two nearest radio masts which act as a guide. The track soon enters a deep gully and after passing a holiday cottage with an amazing array of farm implements incorporated in the gate, continue ahead uphill by a hedgerow filled with birdlife. After passing Upper Hill House, the going steepens, but you can avoid the worst of this by bearing away to the left and then round again to regain the fence higher up.

Turn right before the old quarry (A). On the high ground watch for wheatears, meadow pipits and kestrels, and so arrive at the radio station. Bear right towards a wall with trees beyond it and follow the wall eastwards (to your left) along the hilltop on level ground. Ahead of you is the summit of the hill at 1,790 ft. On a clear day one can see, to the west, the curved profile of Cader Idris, near Dolgellau on the Welsh coast.

Where the wall ends turn left and with your back to the wall walk down the valley which now presents itself. Ignore the inviting paths (D and E), you must

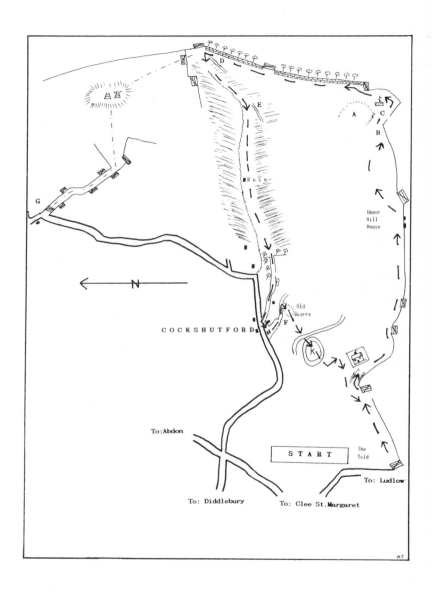

keep to the valley dropping downhill, bearing right at E, eventually passing a ruin and following the stream which is below you to your right.

On reaching the road by some cottages at Cockshutford you will see two field gates. Go through the higher one, pass a house and garage and go to the slabs of concrete, all that remains of the Clee Hill mineral railway trans-shipment station. Turn left, through a wicket gate, and up the incline. At the top are examples of the types of rail used and a few yards further on you will see an actual cutting through which the railway ran.

Where the cutting ends in a quarry, turn right, walking through the quarry and passing grassed over spoil tips to Nordy Bank hill fort. Leave the fort on the south side, from where you can see your car and the path back is self-evident.

Historical Notes

Brown Clee was, at the turn of the 19th century, a centre of industrial activities such as ironstone quarrying, coal mines, and even had its own mineral railway. It does seem odd to find coal seams at such a high altitude yet it was so, making it the highest coalfield in Britain. The ironstone fed forges in the area, one of which one was at Abdon. It is difficult to imagine this lovely hill alive with men, noise and smoke from their fires as they fought to claw a living from the earth. The quarry at A is now just a faint scar in the landscape, but you can still see the coal seams at B. The depressions in the ground at C which look rather like bomb craters are the remains of bell-mines. A miner would first sink a shaft, not very deep, then sit at the bottom and hack away at the coal seam all around him, which, of course, got further away as he worked. Eventually he would get the area around him so wide that the whole thing caved in. The miner would then pack up his tools and move a few yards and start again. What you see are the remains of the caved in workings, called bell-mines on account of their shape.

At the other old quarry at Cockshutford (F), at the top of the incline the wagons would be tipped into buckets on an overhead cable-way for shipment to the road below, from where the ore would be transhipped to the nearest rail-head.

Ludlow is probably Shropshire's most picturesque town. The pride of Ludlow is its castle, but it is also duly noted for its wealth of half-timbered houses among which the Feathers Hotel is the most outstanding. The butter cross stands at the top of Broad Street while a perfectly preserved town gate stands at the bottom, and all are worthy of attention. Ludlow holds a festival every June when, among its attractions, a play by Shakespeare is performed in the open air in the castle grounds.

St Milburga's Well (Stoke St Margaret): St Milburga was Shropshire's own royal saint. The legend is that although she was a very holy and beautiful woman she nevertheless made many enemies and was obliged to live in hiding. Forced to flee she mounted a white horse and, pursued by her foes with a pack of bloodhounds and a gang of rough men, set off south-west. After two days and nights she reached the spot where the well now is and falling in a faint from her horse struck her head on a stone. Men sowing barley in the next field and seeing the blood called for water but there was none, whereupon her horse struck his hoof into the rock, from which a spring gushed forth. Milburga commanded the men to have their sickles ready and instantly the newly sown seed sprang into green shoots. By mid-day it was fully grown and when the pursuers arrived in the evening the men were reaping the ripened crop. When asked if they had seen the saint, the men replied they had when they were sowing the crop and the pursuers want away baffled. It was mid February.

Tugford, Heath and Bouldon

Introduction: This is a pleasant walk through rich agricultural land in a very wide and quiet valley offering superb views. Walking is easy except in wet weather when ploughed fields are apt to be a little sticky due to the clay soil. Excellent views unfold throughout the walk, to the Stretton Hills in the west and the Clee Hills close by to the east. It is a walk of peace and tranquillity with just the wind and birds for company, and a lost medieval village to discover.

Distance: A 3 mile circular walk from Tugford to Heath allowing two and a half hours excluding stops or a 6 mile circular walk from Tugford to Clee St Margaret, taking in Heath and Bouldon. Allow four hours for this longer walk. Map — OS Landranger 137.

Refreshments: None on the route, but there are several inns on the Craven Arms—Bridgnorth road between Aston Munslow and Beambridge.

How to get there: Turn off the Craven Arms to Bridgnorth road (B4368) at Beambridge 1.6 miles north-east of Aston Munslow, as signposted 'Tugford 2'. After 1 mile turn left signed 'Broadstone 1¼' and again after a further ½ mile, turn right now signposted 'Tugford 1¼' and ⅓ mile further on turn right again. Tugford consists of a few houses grouped along its lane and a church accessible by crossing a field. Park anywhere near the church. (GR 557871).

The Walk: Walk south-west away from the church. The lane turns left and by a bungalow with a white sun-lounge is a stile and bridleway sign. The path runs alongside the hedgerow on your left and you continue up this field until you find a wicket gate leading into the woods.

On emerging from the woods, turn half-left across field A heading towards the gap in the tree line where there is a gate into the next field B partially hidden by rising ground. Now go straight up field B which gives superb views to the west across Corvedale to the Stretton Hills, Ragleth and Caradoc to the fore, and the Longmynd dark and lowering beyond. There is a coniferous copse (C) on your left, on the high ground, and another straight ahead. Steer a course between the two to where there is a gap with just three or four lone deciduous trees.

At the corner of the copse bear slightly right (as you arrive) and go straight ahead (there is a wooden electricity pole at D to your left). Keep along the near

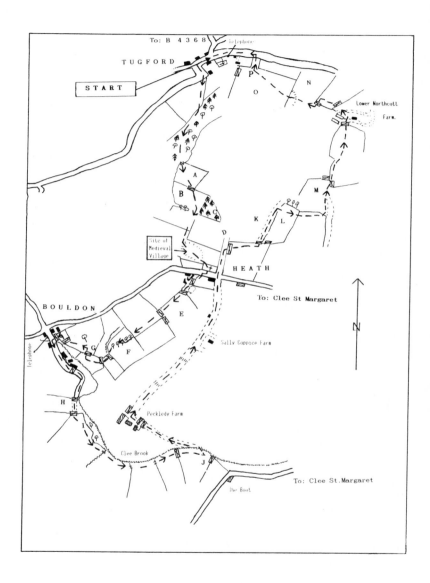

hedgerow and cross the stile near the corner of the field. Continue ahead for a further 10 yards then, where the hedge on the left turns left, do so and you are now entering the lost village of Heath of which the chapel alone survives. The various humps and patterns are all that remains of the foundations of the houses.

Go out of the church gate and turn half-right, crossing the road to the bridleway sign by a wall. Cross the field. and then go through two gates, almost facing each other and skirting round a pond. Turn right in the new field and keep the hedgerow on your right.

There are two gates facing you at the bottom of this field (E). Go through the gate on the right so that the hedge is on your left and keep alongside it to the bottom corner of the field where an apology for a stile enables you to gain access to the next field (F). There are scrubby trees on your right and a wire fence but there are several gaps, go through any one so that the trees are on your left. Go through the gate at the bottom and crossing a stream go through a second, almost facing, gate and walk towards the village of Bouldon just visible ahead of you (hedge on right). Before you get to the stables go through a gate on your right (G) into the next field and head towards the houses which now come into view. Go through two more gates into the village. Turn left at the lane.

Follow the lane past Bouldon Mill and note the mill wheel, not now in use. Beyond that pass Pool Cottage and go uphill to a gate at the start of a narrow track. On your left you can just make out the bed of the old mill race, which was where the water to drive the mill wheel was channelled, rather like a narrow canal. It is visible from the gate for quite a way. Go through the next gate. At (H) the lane soon becomes rather wet so take to the high ground as far as the next gate.

Now bear half-left crossing a long field towards the edge of a fence (I) but there bear slightly right towards the next edge of the field ahead, skirt round a wooded hollow then down the slope and over a side-stream. Continue ahead with Clee Brook on your left, crossing several stiles and side streams until a chimney stack comes into view (J).

Stop and look to your left. There is a footbridge crossing the Clee Brook partially concealed by the bushes and trees. That's your way now. It is the start of a narrow hedged in lane which takes you gently uphill past Peckledy Farm, where turning right you come on a metalled track back to Heath. There are superb views along this lane, the hill in the middle is Hopesay Hill and to its right, in the dim distance, is the flat outline of the Longmynd.

At the crossroads by Heath chapel cross over into the facing lane. Turn right through the first gate on the right and bear slightly left to follow the fence line and trees. Ahead of you is the bulk of Brown Clee Hill topped by its radio masts.

There are three gates out of this field. The third is in the farthest corner, but turn left at the one before onto a muddy field track. In this field (K) there is a round pound surrounded by trees. Stay on this track into the next field until you come nearly to another copse. Turn right through where a gate should be into field L and cross it in a dead straight line heading for a lone tree the other side, at the foot of which is a rather obscure stile. Cross it and continue ahead.

At the corner of the next field the hedge bears gently right and there by a tall tree, turn left and cross through the hedge (no stile) into field M. On your right is a rather overgrown green lane, this part is walkable but difficult and it is better to stay in the field by the hedge (on right). There are two gates at the end of the field, go through the first gate (on your right), so that the hedge is then on your left and keep it so until joining the track to Lower Northcott Farm.

Go through the gate by a red-brick barn, turn right and cross the track to a wicket gate. Turn left, pass a black barn and cross the metalled track to a field gate beyond. Now continue ahead. The next stile out of field N is obscured by the high ground but it is up to your left. Another ancient track can be made out in field O and this leads towards Tugford, now visible through the trees. At the bottom head for the church but watch the stream and when it bears right at P turn right with it and you will, in just a few steps, see a footbridge. Turn left in the lane to return to the village.

Historical Notes

Heath: There are within England some 2,263 known lost villages and this walk explores one of them. Heath stands on high ground on the east side of Corvedale and is now just a field marked by humps. Why did this village die? One theory is that the people were driven out by the monastic houses of the 12th century or another that the villagers were driven off the land by the Enclosures Act. All that now remains is the church, the doorway of which is Norman, and it has an unusual choir gallery and 14th century east window. The key can be obtained from a nearby farm.

Ancient tracks: This walk has taken in many of the old tracks, or 'straker ways' to give them their local name, that abound in this part of Shropshire. They derive from old drove roads by which the villagers, or commoners, drove their cattle onto the Clee Hill for grazing. At J you may have noticed how the track from Peckledy stops at the brook, which appears from there to be the track under water. This is probably what it is for farther on the track re-appears on the other side of the brook. At Clee St Margaret the entire road is under water.

Corvedale

NOT WHEN WET (PTO)

Introduction: Corvedale is described by Lawrence Garner in his Shire County Book to Shropshire as 'the least spoilt in Shropshire' and this is certainly true. It is a scattering of hamlets situated among rich farmland, neat fields and isolated woods, and watched over by the mass of Brown Clee Hill to the east and the lesser but longer incline of Wenlock Edge to the west. This is a walk of peacefulness with a feeling of being 'far from the madding crowd', but there is also a surprise — a piece of the Great Wall of China!

Distance: 4 miles, allow three hours with plenty of time to stop and stare. Map — OS Landranger 137.

Refreshments: The Swan Inn at the start of the walk and where, if you partake of refreshments, you may be able to park with the landlord's permission.

How to get there: Aston Munslow is mid-way between Craven Arms and Bridgnorth on the B4368. Find somewhere off the main road, in the village, to park, where you won't cause any obstruction. (GR 512868).

The Walk: Leaving your car and with the B4368 behind you, walk through the village and fork right at the entrance to the White House Folk Museum. The lane climbs slowly but steadily before turning right and levelling off. This is but a brief respite and take advantage of it to admire the view to the east. That's the Brown Clee Hill the other side.

Halfway along the lane with Little London Farm in front of you, turn left at the bridleway sign and take to a wide grassy track going again gently uphill towards the woods. In autumn bring a spare bag for this blackberry country.

On breasting the hill, take one last look back before bearing right into the woods. The path is easy to follow and drops gently downhill very quickly emerging from the woods to give you now extensive views in the other direction. You are now looking to the west, first to Wenlock Edge and beyond that to the Stretton Hills, Ragleth and Caradoc and behind them the long, flat outline of the Longmynd.

Continue downhill through two fields to remote Wetmoor Farm. Turn right at the gate before the farm sheds and cross the field on the level to a second gate. This leads into Little London Woods where a wide and clear track winds steadily uphill. It can be muddy at times.

After a further mile, you will find yourself round the east side of the hill again with the occasional glimpse eastwards to Brown Clee Hill. Where the path widens considerably and there are extensive blackberry bushes you come

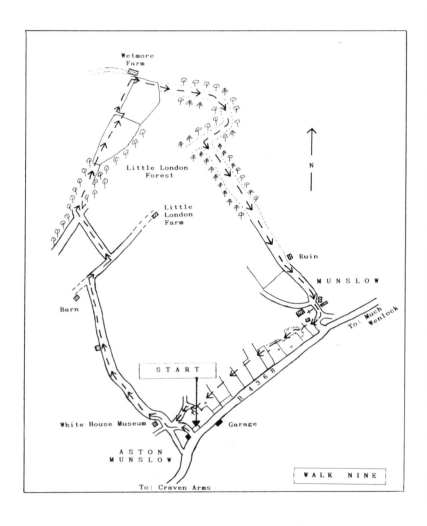

to a T junction of grassy tracks. Turn left here (east) onto a track dropping slowly downhill with a conifer plantation on your right. Follow this until you come out of the woods with clear views across to Brown Clee Hill straight ahead.

Just past some ruins (on the left) come to a gate. The track now drops downhill steeply through a deep cutting and takes you directly to Munslow. However, in wet weather, this track can be dangerous as much of it is made up of limestone slabs which can be very slippery. If you don't want to risk it, turn right at the gate and follow the hedge line (on your left) through two fields until you see below you a metalled road which doubles back to Munslow.

The 'Great Wall of China' is here, in the church, just inside the door and used as a door-stop!

Return to Aston Munslow by turning right outside the church and right again at the first road junction. In about 10 yards go through a gate with the name 'Alcroft' on it. Don't be surprised to find yourself crossing somebody's front lawn. The path then continues beside the hedge over a stone bridge and a stile. Now go straight up to the tree topped hill. At the next gate go straight ahead (hedge on left) and over a stile (hedge now on right) then by a succession of stiles, cross seven more fields keeping straight ahead all the time, with superb views across Corvedale until you arrive back at Aston Munslow. Turn right in the lane by the chapel and then left for the centre of the village and left again to return to the Swan Inn.

Historical Notes

Aston Munslow's claim to fame is The White House Museum, which has won several prizes in its time and appeared on television. It is well worth a visit. The Swan Inn is a lovely building and repute has it that Dick Turpin stayed here, but show me an inn where he didn't stay! The Crown Inn is situated on the main road south of the village and is of interest once having been a Hundred House.

Munslow church: The stone from the Great Wall of China was brought back in 1884 by Lt Edmund P. Powell, RN and is probably the only example of its kind in this country. The tower of the church is late Norman, the chancel is 12th century, early English and the nave 13th to 15th century. The splendid timber-framed south porch is unusual and the style of carving dates it as 14th century. A fully detailed leaflet about the church is available inside.

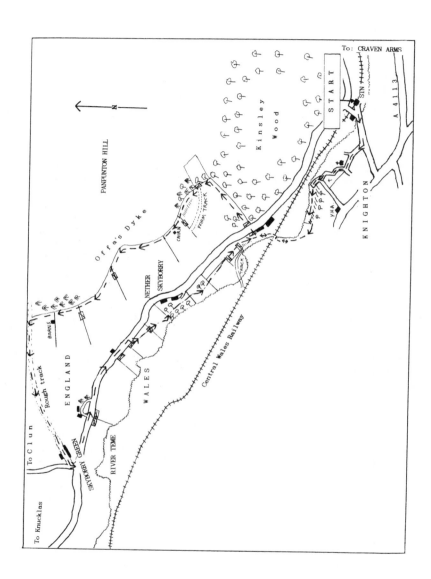

Knighton
and Offa's Dyke

Introduction: Knighton is unique in that its railway station is in England while the town itself is in Wales, a truly 'border town'. The walk starts at the railway station and after a level walk alongside the river Teme which forms the actual frontier, there is a short climb to the hill on the north side of the town where stretches of Offa's Dyke are clearly seen, and which gives stupendous views ahead. The Teme meandering through the rich low-lying meadows leads the eye to the graceful Knucklas Viaduct with the backdrop westwards of distant hills. This is buzzard country and the cry of these beautiful birds can be heard far and wide. This ramble has been planned to go westwards so that the ever changing view makes it a walk to remember.

Distance: The Knighton round walk is 5 miles, allow three and a half hours. If you want to return to Knighton by train, 4 miles Knighton to Knucklas, allow three hours (excluding stops). The only climb is from the railway to Offa's Dyke on the outward leg. Map — OS Landranger 137.

Refreshments: Cafés, hotels and pubs in Knighton, one right opposite the railway station. There are picnic tables by the river where there is also a car park (see map) and a viewpoint with seat by the cairn overlooking the valley (see map).

How to get there: By car from Shrewsbury take the A49 south through Church Stretton and turn right at Craven Arms for Clun; bear left for Leintwardine and right at Clungunford for Bucknell. Left at Bucknell, over the railway to the A4113, turn right for Knighton. On entering, in sight of the clock tower, turn right into Station Road and park at the station. By train — take the Swansea line train from Shrewsbury, Church Stretton or Craven Arms, to Knighton. (GR 290725).

The Walk: Leave the station yard and turn left into Station Road alongside the Teme and crossing into Wales. Turn first right into Church Street (no name), pass the church and turn right into Cemetery Road which ends at the Offa's Dyke car park (where you can park if you prefer). Continue ahead by a paved path which then enters a field. Cross the river and the railway and bear away from the river to the gate by the barns.
  Cross the lane and go through the gate opposite. This is the only climb on the walk so take your time. At the top turn left as signposted and keeping close

73

to the fence (on right) go up another short slope (ignoring side tracks) to the stile at the top. Although it is not very pronounced this is Offa's Dyke, and the views ahead are breath-taking. At the head of the valley you will see the beautiful Knucklas Viaduct by which the railway crosses the valley. Continue along Offa's Dyke path negotiating several stiles until you come to a gritty track going left to right across your path. Turn left down the track and follow it out to the road in the valley below. Turn left.

At the road junction, *turn right for Knucklas* if you came by train or want a lift back to Knighton and follow the lane as signposted 'Llanfair Waterdine 2'. In ½ mile, turn left at signpost 'Knighton 3'. At the main road, A4113, turn left, there is a wide grass verge to walk on. Ignore the lane opposite with sign 'Knucklas' and go on for another 200 yards to the next turning right. Turn right into Knucklas here and in just a few yards, turn left into 'Glyndwyr' and the station is dead ahead.

To return to Knighton turn left, and walk back along the lane passing Skyborry Farm. One hundred yards after a modern bungalow, on your left, is a field gate on your right. Go through and fork left across the field keeping near the hedge as a guide. Through a second gate, cross the field, making for the far right-hand corner where there is a sort of stile. Into the woods now and what seems an old drove road, flat and grassy with just one tricky spring to negotiate at the start. Keep to the right of the white garage and in the field beyond fork right down a slope. At the bottom keep straight on over a fence into the next field and up the rise in front. Go through the next gate and keep straight on. Through the next gate and down another slope and there you are, back at the railway bridge. By retracing your steps return to the station.

Historical Notes

Knighton is in the extreme south-west corner of Shropshire and straddles the English/Welsh Border. The dyke was constructed by King Offa in the 8th century when he ruled Mercia. Mercia covered the area of the Midlands from the Welsh Border to East Anglia and from the Humber to the Thames. The Dyke stretches for 140 miles along the border from Chepstow in the south to Prestatyn in the north and was opened as a long distance footpath in 1970 by one of its foremost champions, Lord Hunt of Everest who still has a cottage in the area. It is a footpath of ever changing scenes and of great beauty and Knighton is about half-way along it. The dyke acted as a frontier between Offa's kingdom and Wales. Like so many Border towns its architecture has examples of the half-timbered black and white houses which give the streets an air of ageless beauty. The clock tower in the market place is a focal point. The Welsh name is Trefyclawdd, meaning 'The town on the dyke'.

Central Wales Line: Work began at Craven Arms in August 1861 and the line opened on 10th October 1865. Originally used extensively for freight it is now a passenger-only line and having survived many closure attempts much money has been spent in improvement in the last few years.

The Knucklas Viaduct came about as a result of the intransigent attitude of the local landowner whose castle overlooked the valley. He did not want his view spoilt so, instead of building the line on the north side of the Teme which was the logical place, it had to be built on the south side involving the construction of several extra bridges and the viaduct, which the owner stipulated had to have castle-like towers at both sides. The castle itself is no more but the viaduct is one of the highlights of the line.

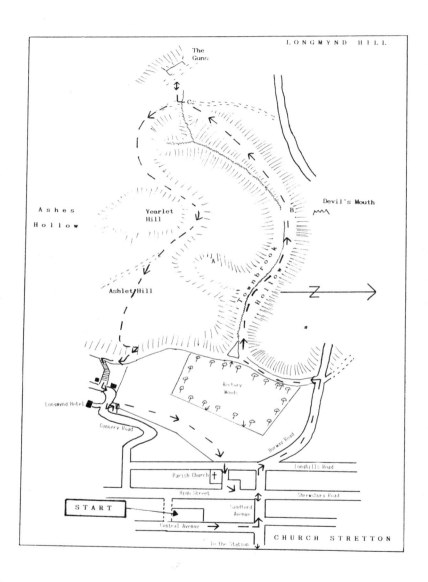

LONGMYND HILL

The Guns

Cr

Ashes
Hollow

Yearlet
Hill

Devil's Mouth

B

Ashlet Hill

A

Townbrook Hollow

N

Rectory
Woods

Longmynd Hotel

Cunnery Road

Burway Road

Longhills Road

Parish Church

High Street

Shrewsbury Road

Sandford
Avenue

START

Central Avenue

To the Station

CHURCH STRETTON

Church Stretton and The Guns

Introduction: Church Stretton and its surrounding hills is a natural area to which walkers gravitate. At week-ends the town is crowded with visitors but away in the hills one can wander 'lonely as a cloud' even on the busiest bank holiday. This walk visits the most unlikely of sites for an area of outstanding natural beauty, an old artillery range. There are superb views on the return leg from Ashlet Hill.

Distance: 4 miles, allow three hours plus stops. The upper part of the valley is steep but gradual; the grassy descent can be slippery in wet weather and good walking shoes or boots are advisable. Map — OS Landranger 137.

Refreshments: Plenty of cafés and pubs in Church Stretton, and fresh sandwiches and cooked meats from the bakers (open Sundays).

How to get there: Church Stretton is 13 miles south of Shrewsbury and north of Ludlow on the A49 trunk road. It is also served by a good rail service. Park in the Central Avenue car park (it is well signposted). (GR 455935).

The Walk: Leave the car park and turn left. Turn left again into Sandford Avenue. Go straight across at Lloyds Bank into Burway Road which you follow as far as the cattle grid. Turn left at the cattle grid and take the level grassy track which runs alongside Rectory Woods. Bear right by the reservoir and follow the valley for a mile.

Where the valley suddenly bends left, by two gnarled hawthorn trees (B) and with the Devil's Mouth rock towering above, you will find a narrow track cut into the hillside and bearing away from the stream. Follow this new track which gently rises for about a mile until it levels out at the head of the valley.

There are no obvious signs to point you now as we are out on the plateau of the Longmynd, but you are at point C on the sketch map. To find 'The Guns' follow the map. There are some sheep tracks through the heather going uphill, with a gully as a guide. The road is away in the distance to your right. After ten minutes or so, the gully levels off at a bog and beyond that there is more heather and then a wide track. 'The Guns' were here overlooking Ashes Hollow and if you look carefully you will be able to see the flat squares where the guns once stood, as well as planks of wood and indeed one or two bolts which secured the guns.

Now return to the head of Townbrook Hollow and turning right follow the narrow but well defined track which bears round the left-hand side of the hill. As you round Yearlet Hill the view opens out and you are presented with a splendid vista of the Stretton Valley. Continuing on, you pass close to a side valley and point A. The large hole is the result of an underground explosion. In July 1970 a violent thunderstorm deposited over an inch of rain in one hour. There was a bog here which being unable to absorb the torrent of water pouring into it from underground springs exploded, sending tons of soil into the valley. It would have been a most impressive sight for anyone fortunate enough to have seen it, and survived! To this day the hole has never revegetated and remains an ugly scar on the hillside.

Now watch carefully for a low small rocky outcrop on the left of the path. Here turn left and follow a very narrow path through the bilberries keeping Townbrook Hollow on your left, and heading towards a ridge. Once on the ridge you will soon see below you the town again and also, a good landmark, the large white edifice of the Longmynd Hotel. A wide grassy track leads downhill heading directly towards it.

You will end up by a fence. Turn right for 10 yards to a stile and then down the 'hundred steps' and out to the road. Turn left into Cunnery Road for 100 yards until you come to the entrance to Rectory Fields (small car park, field gate and wicket gate). Walk straight down the field, which brings you out by the parish church. Continue ahead into High Street and the Market Square. Turn left then right into Sandford Avenue and so back to your car or the station.

Historical Notes

The Guns, as it is known, was a firing range used by the Shropshire and South Staffordshire Yeomanry until the early part of the 20th century. The range was situated on the other side of Ashes Hollow on what is called Round Hill, and even today shells can still be found but, I hasten to add, they are quite harmless. The range was closed down when new long-range guns came into use and started to lob shells on the village at Minton, which rather upset the villagers.

Yearlet Hill: The names given to the hills, such as Yearlet, date back to the days when the hill was grazed by cattle. Each had its own particular area, this hill being for yearlings, while, if you look at a map, you will see other names, Cow Ridge, Calf Ridge etc.

Rectory Woods is open to the public. Points of access are shown on the sketch map by small arrows. A nature trail guide is available in local bookshops.

The Market Square: The town was given its market charter by King John in 1214. Market Day is Thursday. There have been two market halls on this spot. The first was in Tudor style, rather like that at Ledbury, but was pulled down in Victorian times and replaced with a red-brick structure which itself was pulled down during the 1960s and an open square left instead. This gives an open area for the market and emphasis to the architectural beauty of the buildings which surround it.

Ashes Hollow

Introduction: The Longmynd Hill is some 10 miles long by 4 miles wide and cut into on its eastern side by deep well-watered valleys, batches or hollows as we call them. Ashes Hollow is a typical example of the Longmynd Valley at its best. Starting on level ground with fields it soon changes its character and becomes a narrow and sometimes difficult valley where the path has been worn away by the swiftly running stream. Despite its closeness to habitation, it retains its remoteness and tranquillity on even the busiest summer days. The may trees in spring are a delight.

Distance: 5 miles for the full walk, reduced to 3 miles if the short cut from Ashes Valley to Pole Cottage is taken. Allow five or six hours and bring a picnic. Map — OS Landranger 137.

Refreshments: The Ragleth Inn and the Green Dragon are both recommended and have gardens for children.

Parking: Only with the landlord's permission, there may be parking available at the inns. There is limited parking on the lane behind the Ragleth, or near the railway line.

How to get there: See walk 18 for directions to Church Stretton. Little Stretton is 1½ miles south of Church Stretton. There is a bus every two hours, but no train, or it is a pleasant level walk from Church Stretton. (GR 455935).

The Walk: Start from (A) the lane behind the stream, turning left at the footbridge. Cross the stile by the public footpath sign, and go ahead through two fields until you come to the National Trust sign. Turn right over the footbridge and then left. Now it's a case of following the stream.

Note at B what appear to be tracks in the ground which suddenly end at the stream. They are indeed old cart tracks for at E (see map) is an old quarry and in those days the stream was the other side of the valley. Over the years it has changed its course and has eaten away the old track. The pile of loose stones at C was washed down the side valley during a violent thunderstorm in July 1970.

The valley narrows now and crossing the stream is required on several occasions. At D there is no path at all and some scrambling is required, though it is not dangerous and should pose no problems to the average walker. You can avoid this narrow section by climbing up the quarry at E from where a level path takes you to the junction at F.

79

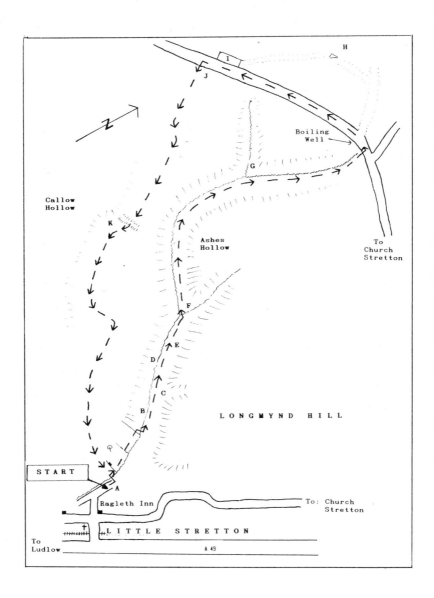

At F take the left fork and this soon opens out into a new and wider valley of quite different character. Heather clad hills to the left are in stark contrast to the ferns and grass to the right. It depends on the soil, where the soil is deep ferns can grow, but where it is shallow only heather can find anchorage.

At G the side valley would take you directly to Pole Cottage. At the top of the valley join the road at Boiling Well. (If you walked to Little Stretton from Church Stretton and want to cut the ramble short, turn right and follow the road as signposted back to Church Stretton.) Otherwise, turn left and keep on the road for just over a mile until you come to the picnic site at Pole Cottage (I). If you wish to visit the summit, follow the rough track from Boiling Well and turn left along the brow on the hill; the path goes over the summit (H) and down to Pole Cottage. Otherwise continue along the road, passing Pole Cottage, until you come to a wide track on the left (J) signposted to Little Stretton, turn left and follow the track. It is well defined and needs no description except to draw your attention to the view into Callow Hollow and the double ditches at (K), remnants of a prehistoric fortification.

Historical Notes

The quarry was used to produce stone for house building but fell into disuse well over a hundred years ago.

Pole Cottage got its name from the 'pole', long since removed, which was erected by the Ordnance Survey about 100 years ago to mark the summit of the plateau. It has now been replaced by a topograph erected in 1986 by the Council for the Protection of Rural England. Close by is the Ordnance Survey trig point.

Pole Cottage was a real cottage, standing in the area where now the National Trust has made a picnic area. It was used for many years by a hermit, then a bee keeper, and during the war by the RAF for falcon training. After that it fell into disuse apart from the grouse shoots in the autumn. Motorised vandals reduced it to ruins. It was bulldozed into the ground by the National Trust as being unsafe.

The duck ponds: Behind the cottage and scattered along the length of the plateau, are several man made duck ponds, created by the last lord of the manor to attract ducks to the area to increase the shooting.

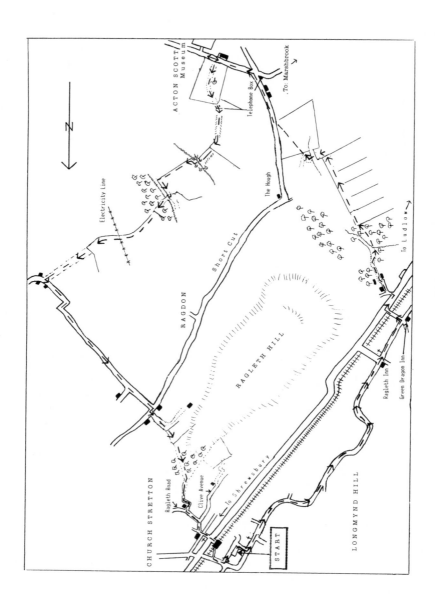

Acton Scott Farm Museum

Introduction: This is a superb walk. Once across the A49 at Little Stretton you will find every footpath signposted and waymarked and every stile in immaculate order. The walk is easy, mostly on the level with peaceful and widespread views over the surrounding country. Farming is predominantly sheep, with some cattle and crops, but there is a never ending change of vista. The Farm Museum is an actual farm worked in the Victorian way and is a fascinating focus for the walk.

Distance: 6 miles, allow four hours for walking, all day if you visit the Farm Museum. Map — OS Landranger 137.

Refreshments: Hot and cold meals at the museum and inns at Little Stretton. Wide choice in Church Stretton.

How to get there: See walk 18 for directions to Church Stretton. There is a good rail service. Park in the Central Avenue car park. (GR 455935).

The Walk: Starting from the car park, find the narrow exit in the south-west corner and turn right into a narrow alley which emerges into the High Street by the King's Arms. Turn left and follow the road to Little Stretton.
Pass the Ragleth Inn and the famous black and white church (on the left), and take the next turning left (almost opposite The Green Dragon). Cross the A49 and turn right then first left into a lane, bearing right by the cottages. The lane goes up a slight hill, at the top of which is a gate; just before that on your right is a slightly obscured stile. Over the stile follow the path alongside a field fence and through the woods, crossing a footbridge and emerging into a field. Now following the hedge line (on the left) continue ahead through five fields to a gate by a water trough. Turn left. Go through the facing gate, over the stream, and turn right uphill to a waymarked stile. Branch half-left over rising ground in the field until you get to the gate in the corner. Turn right along the lane. At the next crossroads, turn left for the museum.
When you have completed your visit to the museum, turn left back the way you came to the first gate on the right (opposite the entrance to Acton Scott Farm; the path is waymarked with a blue arrow (bridleway). Follow the track across the field heading towards Ragleth Hill. In the left-hand corner is a gate and stile and beyond that another gate and a wicket, all waymarked. Through the wicket you walk along a sunken track for a little way to emerge on high ground giving a superb view of Ragleth Hill. Through the next gate with Ragleth on your left and Ragdon Farm half-left, drop downhill to a footbridge.

Cross the bridge and follow the edge of the field to your right. Pass the first gate where you turn left and so to the second gate. Turn right into the woods, and go uphill. At the top of the slope is a field gate. Continue ahead to Chelmick. There are excellent views along this stretch.

Turn left at Chelmick (ignore the blue arrow pointing right) and follow the lane, very little used by vehicles, for a mile, passing a T junction with a letter box by it, and with Ragleth Hill directly ahead. At the next T junction turn right but only for 10 yards, for you now turn left into a farm drive with the name Dryhill.

Go through the first gate, but where the lane bears left continue ahead through a second gate and up a short hill to the third gate. (Ragleth Hill is now to your left and if you wish to climb it on another occasion reverse the instructions from this point on.) The path continues on the level with the fence on the right, gradually dropping downhill through a bluebell wood. The path is quite clear and eventually emerges into Ragleth Road by a bungalow. Turn left to return to the town crossing the A49 by the railway station and into Sandford Avenue. Turn left into Central Avenue to return to the car park.

Historical Notes

The Acton Scott Working Farm Museum was opened in 1975 and is now looked upon as a genuine example of mid-Victorian farming in action. It preserves a way of life now long forgotten, how farming was before the arrival of modern machinery and the internal combustion engine. It is a great favourite with children and an ideal family day out. All the animals are accessible for children to see and touch and demonstrations of butter making, thatching, ploughing, cider making etc are held each week-end throughout the summer. Various farm grown and farm made products can be purchased at the shop. The old school house is now used as a café. There are a variety of walks around the farm and across the fields on well marked footpaths (telephone enquiries Marshbrook 06946-306).

Ragleth Hill offers superb views from its southern end. Unlike the Longmynd which is a wide flat plateau, Ragleth is narrow and steeply sided so that it offers great views to those with the energy to climb it. From the viewpoint you look south to the Black Mountains of Gwent, east to the Brown Clee, Titterstone Clee and Wenlock Edge. Beyond them are the Malvern Hills in Worcestershire. On a very clear day one can also see beyond even them, the low dark outline of the Cotswolds. Immediately below is Little Stretton behind which the Longmynd rears up and blots out views further west, while to the north Caradoc and Lawley complete the picture.

Church Stretton, Cardington and Caradoc

Introduction: Cardington, set in beautiful surroundings, has the reputation of being the loveliest of Shropshire villages. The walk takes in a variety of soft fields, bluebell woods and wild lonely hill tops, with ancient Caradoc as the focus with its great hill fort. Excellent views are possible throughout the walk in every direction.

Distance: 7 miles. Allow five hours. Map — OS Landranger 137.

Refreshments: The Royal Oak, Cardington, or in Church Stretton.

How to get there: See walk 18 for directions to Church Stretton. Start from the Central Avenue car park. (GR 455935).

The Walk: Turn left into Central Avenue, and right into Sandford Avenue. Cross the road to the left-hand side and passing the fire station, turn left into Essex Road.

Turn right at Windsor Court as signposted, and crossing the railway, continue ahead to the A49 road. Cross the A49 and follow the footpath sign. The lane you cross to the stile opposite is part of the original Watling Street. Walk across the field to the stile where the houses end and turn left.

Ignore a narrow lane on the right by a bungalow but turn right at a gate just alongside in the field; it is signed. Follow the path around the edge of the field by the sunken track. This is the old Cardington Road.

Enter woods between Caradoc (left) and Helmeth Woods (right). Where the track dips down to the stream turn right uphill to a wicket gate. Go through. The entrance to Helmeth Woods, now owned by the Woodland Trust and open to the public, is here, and you can come back another day if you wish to walk round it. Continue uphill alongside Helmeth Woods, which spill over into the field.

At the top of the hill turn left alongside a field fence. Go through the gate, cut across the next field to another gate and turn left along the western side of Hope Bowdler Hill. Follow the path on the level along the valley floor, finally turning right uphill near a crossing fence. At the stile at the top turn left onto Willstone Hill.

At this point (A), if you want an easy and shorter walk, turn right instead of left and follow the wide grassy track across the hill and down into Hope Bowdler. Turn right along the road then right again by a barn (waymarked) and

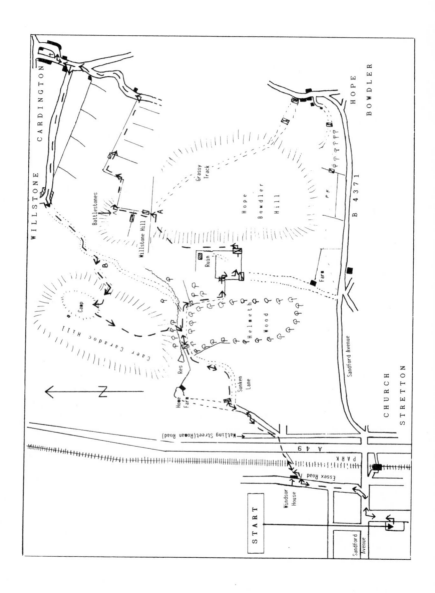

follow the track which later becomes indistinct but runs parallel with the road. In the last field head half-left towards the lamp-post in the far corner and re-enter Church Stretton along Sandford Avenue.

Continuing on the main route, walk north now along the ridge until the fence turns right, downhill; before following it, bear left over the ridge to see the view from the Battlestones. On a clear day Shrewsbury is easily seen and its many church spires, as well as the tall clock tower on the Market Hall. To the west is the tall white blob of the Shelton water tower. Now return to the fence and drop downhill towards the fields below. Over a stile, and turn left along the edge of a field.

Continue ahead at a stile until you come to the lane. Turn left and follow the lane downhill to Cardington. The church is in the centre of the village; for the Royal Oak take the lane round to the right of the church.

The return walk starts from the church and you retrace your steps as far as the first turning right, signposted Willstone. At Willstone, which is just two farms on a right-hand bend, turn left onto a dirt track between banks. This is the old Cardington Road again and if you wish to avoid the climb onto Caradoc you can follow it all the way back to Church Stretton.

At B turn right, through the gate and uphill towards Caradoc. The track is quite clear and leads gently up the hillside to emerge on the ridge right by the camp, which is worth exploring. The view from here down into the Stretton Valley is superb.

To continue back to Church Stretton, which you can see below you, looking along the ridge, walk along the ridge path and down the southern slope. It can be slippery. There is a stile and then you drop down to the stream to rejoin the outward walk, crossing a footbridge and turning right to retrace your steps home.

Historical Notes

Caradoc: Its ancient camp is the subject of great speculation by historians and vies with Hereford Beacon in the Malvern Hills as King Caractacus's last stronghold against the invading Romans. This does seem the more likely of the two contenders since the Roman Centurion Ostorius Scapula, with whom Caractacus did battle, was stationed at nearby Viroconium. The area of houses below the southern end of Caradoc is called 'Battlefield' where, it is reputed, the battle took place in AD 50. On the west side of the hill, just below the summit is a cave said to be where Caractacus took shelter. In the corner of the Caradoc camp is a spring, now rather choked by weed. The area enclosed by the triple ditches is six acres. In the 19th century 'wakes' were held here on Trinity Sunday, tea was made with the spring water and a barrel of beer rolled up.

Cardington: The church lies in the centre of the village surrounded by clusters of very attractive old stone and half-timbered cottages. The building is dedicated to St James and was first built in the 11th century. Beyond the church is the Old School, now a private house which overlooks the Royal Oak, reputed to be one of the oldest licensed houses in England. Opposite the entrance to the church is Maltster's Tap with an interesting longhouse barn dating from 1558, few of which remain.

Watling Street is an old Roman road which ran from Wroxeter to Kenchester just west of Hereford. Several stretches of it are preserved and walkable while others form modern roads. North of Church Stretton, Watling Street is a road and can be driven along for several miles until the approach to Acton Burnell.

Hope Bowdler church dates back to the 12th century, the present building being 17th century. For such a small parish it has a remarkable peal of bells. It is set in most picturesque surroundings and the churchyard is approached by an avenue of yew trees which is quite unique and was planted in 1860.

WALK TWENTY TWO

Ratlinghope and
The Darnford Valley

Introduction: This is a fascinating walk steeped in ancient history. On the west side of the Longmynd, between it and the sinister outline of the Stiperstones, is a hidden valley known as Darnford. It is an area rich in folklore and legend and includes the Port Way, a prehistoric track littered with burial mounds. The walk starts with soft woods and meadows and a clear rushing stream, so beloved of lowland birds, and later changes to the harsher upland areas of heather, gorse and bracken with all the attendant changes in wildlife that go with it.

Distance: 6½ miles or 8½ miles. Allow four hours for the short walk and five for the long walk. Map — OS Landranger 137.

Refreshments: The Bridges Inn.

How to get there: Bridges lies on an unclassified road running south-west from Shrewsbury through Longden and Pulverbatch (with a castle mound and excellent inn, The White Horse). Shortly after passing Ratlinghope post office you will see a large board welcoming you to the Bridges Inn. It is slightly north-west of Church Stretton, the nearest market town and railway, and there is a youth hostel. Park on the road opposite the Bridges Inn. (GR 395965).

The Walk: From the inn turn right, signposted Church Stretton, and walk past the youth hostel until you come to a narrow bridge just before which, on your left, is a gate and stile with the words 'Shropshire Way' carved into it. The way up the valley as far as the Port Way is now easy to follow being waymarked by Shropshire Way signs depicting a buzzard with wings outspread.

At the end of the wood, just before a packhorse bridge fork left, over a stile and cross the field heading for the woods. The path through is easy to follow. On emerging go straight over a track and continue ahead following the Shropshire Way signs.

By a red-brick cottage (opposite) turn left on a rough track which soon becomes grassy and is clear all the way to Lower Darnford. From the first gate you can see the outline of the ancient British camp (A) and can walk up to it by the side valley (on your left) after passing through the gate. Over the years a number of ancient tools have been found together with some Roman coins. Continue up the valley ignoring any side tracks.

89

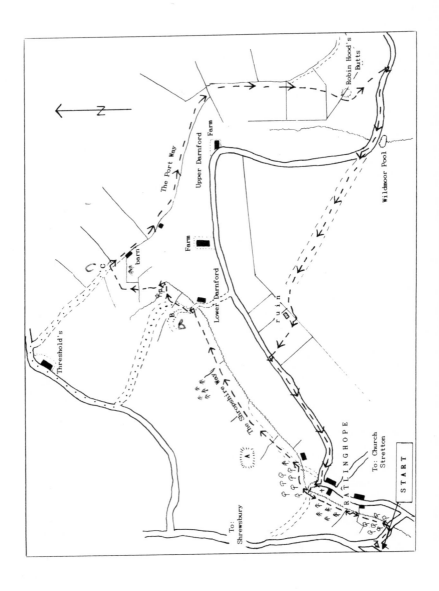

Lower Darnford is a converted farmhouse on the other side of the stream. By the footpath signpost pointing back towards Bridges turn left uphill and go through the next gate with another Shropshire Way signpost (no stile). Ignoring the track going uphill (left) continue ahead on the level to the gate/stile directly in front. Here (B) the long and short walks divide.

Long walk: From B turn left and follow the farm track which goes left uphill eventually becoming a track. When you come to the road, turn right for ¼ mile and after passing Threshold's Farm, turn right onto the Port Way. Walk along this until you rejoin the short walk at C — there is a gate in front and a Shropshire Way signpost by the gate on the right.

Short walk: Continue ahead as signposted, heading for the right-hand side of the lines of trees in the valley. It is best to keep to the right of the former field boundary, now just a linear lump, as otherwise it gets very boggy. There is a footbridge over the stream and then ahead another signpost. By following the path and further Shropshire Way signs you wind your way uphill and then through a rather long and steeply sided field to the Port Way. Turn right (C). *Long-walk walkers rejoin here.*

Go through the gate. Here the track is partially metalled but this soon ends. Pass the barn and the Ordnance Survey trig. point still keeping straight ahead and with wide views north across the Shropshire Plain. In the middle distance you can see the low flat outline of Haughmond Hill while nearer to your right is the volcanic outline of the Wrekin. This field ends in a funnel between two fences at the end of which is a gate. Continue ahead along the ridge path with a farm below you in the valley and the bracken of the Longmynd beyond.

The first field is rather long, but after passing through the gate and passing another 'milestone' (in fact a parish boundary marker stone), breast the rising ground. You will now see, ahead of you, another field. Keep this, and the two trees you can see, in mind for on passing through the next gate the Port Way has been ploughed out and the farm track bearing away left is not the way to go. Try to keep straight on, in line with the track behind you and the two trees ahead. There is no clearly defined path. Clearing the rising ground look out for the outline of a former field boundary, again another linear lump, but making two sides of a triangle. Keep some distance to the right of this and very soon you will see the field fence on your right and another ahead with a gate close to which is a stile. Ahead of you is the Longmynd with its heather and bracken and the unmistakable hump of Robin Hood's Butts. After crossing a second short field go through the last gate (no stile) and there the Port Way is again a wide track.

On reaching the road turn right. Wildmoor Pool is now, alas, so silted up with reeds that one might almost pass it without realising it is a pond. Just beyond is a wide dirt track forking left off the road signposted Ratlinghope. Walk along this track until you come to a field and a gate by a ruined barn. Cross the field, downhill, towards a line of trees at the end of which is a gate into the lane. Turn left and so back to Ratlinghope.

Take the second turning on the right, just by the church. After passing a barn and a cottage, cross a footbridge and turn left into the woods to retrace your steps to the starting point.

Historical Notes

The Port Way is a prehistoric track running the length of the Longmynd and walkable throughout. On either side are burial mounds. The track would have been of prime importance as it avoided the marshy and densely wooded lowland valleys, which is why we find so many camps or settlements on the high ground. In more recent times the track was used by people from Bishops Castle as a main route to Shrewsbury before the coming of motor vehicles. The track can, in fact, be followed beyond our walk. From Threshold's Farm it continues north past the stone in the middle of the field, eventually becoming the present day road from Pulverbatch to Shrewsbury. At the south end of the Longmynd it also becomes a lane to Bishops Castle.

Ratlinghope is pronounced 'Rah-chup' and the name means 'the valley of the children of Rotel'. It is perhaps one of the oddest places in England. Here in Darnford Valley is the manor house, which you can see across the field from the woods, and the church, while the rest of the village and the post office are a couple of miles away the other side of the hills to your left, on the road from Shrewsbury.

Ghosts: Ghosts seem to crop up just about anywhere in Shropshire, but especially around the Longmynd and the Stiperstones. If you drove to Bridges from Church Stretton you would have passed the site of the former shooting box which was situated on the Port Way. One day two ladies from the Congregational church in Church Stretton were walking. There was no metalled road in those days so they would have walked up Cardingmill Valley where one of the ladies lived. As they walked past the shooting box, Miss Widdowson stood to one side to allow a horseman to pass. Her friend wondered what she was doing and Miss Widdowson, surprised, replied that she had stood to one side to let the rider pass. But her friend had seen no rider! The legend about this rider, who is called 'Wild Edric', is that he and his followers sleep under the Stiperstones and come out when the nation is in danger, and that he will be seen riding in the direction from which the threat is coming. It was 1938 and he was riding in a south-easterly direction, toward Germany! Less than a year later we were at war.
    Further on your walk you will pass Wildmoor Pond and the track between it and Marsh Farm is haunted by a phantom funeral procession.

Robin Hood's Butts: These are ancient burial mounds and very good examples they are. How they got their name is not known, but the legend is that Robin Hood shot an arrow from the butts and hit the church tower at Ludlow, some 15 miles away due south! A more likely explanation may be a connection with one Humphrey Kynaston, Shropshire's own Robin Hood, who led a similar life in the cliffs at Nescliff near Shrewsbury.

Possible

Callow Hollow

Introduction: One of the more southerly, longest and least frequented of the Longmynd valleys is Callow Hollow. A quiet place and one of great beauty, it is not to be missed by those who love solitude. The view of it from its eastern end is quite beautiful. The valley is one of the most open and widest on the hill, which also adds to its attractions. Once on top of the Longmynd you traverse part of the Port Way, then watch the gliders landing and taking off from the Midland Gliding Club, and finally return to your car by an ancient drove road.

Distance: 4½ miles, allow four hours for an easy walk. Map — OS Landranger 137.

Refreshments: The Ragleth and Green Dragon inns, at Little Stretton.

How to get there: See walk 18 for directions to Church Stretton. Take the B4370 south to Little Stretton. Turn right at the Ragleth Inn then left at the next junction, and in a few yards bear right. Continue along a narrow lane for ½ mile to a ford and park just beyond it where the lane widens. (GR 433912).

The Walk: Leave the car and walk along the lane in the same direction, passing two field gates. Just after the second turn right into a small pine wood and follow a wide grassy track uphill until you come to open hillside at Small Batch Valley. Turn right and go up a short slope with the fence on your right. When you get to the top you will have one of the finest views of any Longmynd valley, for from here you can see right up the Callow Hollow until the folds of the hill close in.

The valley is peppered with paths on this, the south side of the valley, and you can choose which to take. In the end they all meet by the stream higher up the valley so it matters not which you use. Assuming you use the path by the stream a little care is needed on the loose stones as you descend into the valley. Turn left and follow the stream.

Whichever path you use, continue up the valley as shown on the map until you reach the end of the valley at (A) where you are virtually out of the valley with only a slight rise on either side and in front. Fork left when you can see two trees ahead of you and where two streams join. Ahead you will soon see a fence on the skyline, by which is the road. Turn left along the road.

This is another portion of the Port Way, here metalled and used by vehicles, but you walk it for only a short distance. On breasting the rise ahead you will see beyond it the gliding field. If you wish to stop and watch, there are plenty of places to do so, but watch out for the winch cable and do not go too close.

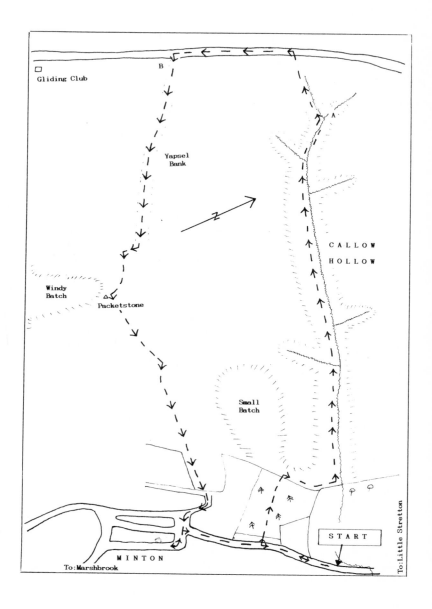

You will see a wide grassy track on your left (B). Turn left along it. This is the old drove road and goes all the way back to Minton though it is less distinct later. On the right you can see the Longmynd Forest. The views open out as you walk up Yapsel Bank. You can see south to Craven Arms and beyond that to Ludlow, the Clee Hills and further still the Black Mountains near Brecon which stretch across the southern horizon. On a clear day the pinnacle of the Sugar Loaf Hill at Abergavenny can be seen.

The track peters out after ½ mile, but from here you can see the Packetstone, a prominent rocky outcrop. Bear slightly right, through the heather towards it and you will soon come upon a narrow footpath skirting round Windy Batch and leading to the Packetstone. From the stone the path runs clear and straight down through the bracken, soon to join a wider track coming from your left. Now continue straight ahead with lovely views over the Stretton Valley. There is Ragleth and Caradoc to your left (north) and Wenlock Edge ahead, capped by Flounders Folly. As you descend into Minton the traces of the old road will become even more marked, at places almost a sunken road, but grassy and dry. The tracks made by cart-wheels can still be seen.

After passing through the gate by the National Trust sign, pass a cottage and turn right on a track which leads to the village green. Turn left. Before turning left again, signposted Little Stretton, go straight ahead at the crossroads into a lane which bears right round the farm. You will see here in front of you the castle mound which is now all that remains of a Norman motte and bailey. Now return to the crossroads and turn right down a narrow lane and back to the start.

Historical Notes

The Longmynd Moor is mostly of heather and bracken and is the most southerly maintained grouse moor in Britain. The grouse, large brown birds with a distinctive chuckling call, are hunted for sport from 'the glorious 12th' August each year and about four to five shoots take place. Many other birds nest on the moor. Snipe is an interesting and uncommon bird, mainly found among marsh grass which it favours, it has no song but instead makes a sound rather reminiscent of a tuneless bassoon. It does this in flight by the use of its tail feathers. Another bird beloved of local folk is the curlew with its evocative song, its long curved beak making it easy to identify.

The Gliding Club is a post-war addition. The road was not made up until after the Second World War. The club attracts a large following and more recently its activities have been added to with the advent of hang gliding. Both sports take root here because of the steep windward facing west slopes which, forcing the prevailing winds to rise, give the necessary lift.

The Packetstone goes back much further into history. In the days before the railways and tarmac roads, most travel was, of course, by horse, and this was a drove road from England into Wales. The story surrounding the Packetstone is that on reaching this point, the drover would stand on the stone in order to adjust the load, or packets, on the pony's back before commencing the descent into Minton, hence the name 'Packet' stone.

Minton Castle: A motte was a banked and palisaded area. It was steep sided, and was sometimes attached to the bailey and sometimes enclosing it. The top was ringed by a palisade with a platform inside, to which wooden steps led up. Inside was a square wooden tower used as an armoury, a watch tower and a refuge. As construction was of wood nothing of it now remains. The bailey contained domestic buildings for horses and food storage. Most such castles were constructed during the 11th and 12th centuries.

Flounder's Folly was built as a look-out in 1839 by Benjamin Flounder and is said to mark the spot where four estates meet. The story is that Flounder built the tower so that he could watch his ships docking in Liverpool, but he must have had very good eyesight!